James H. Rubin

NADAR 55

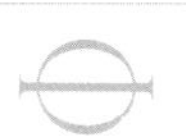

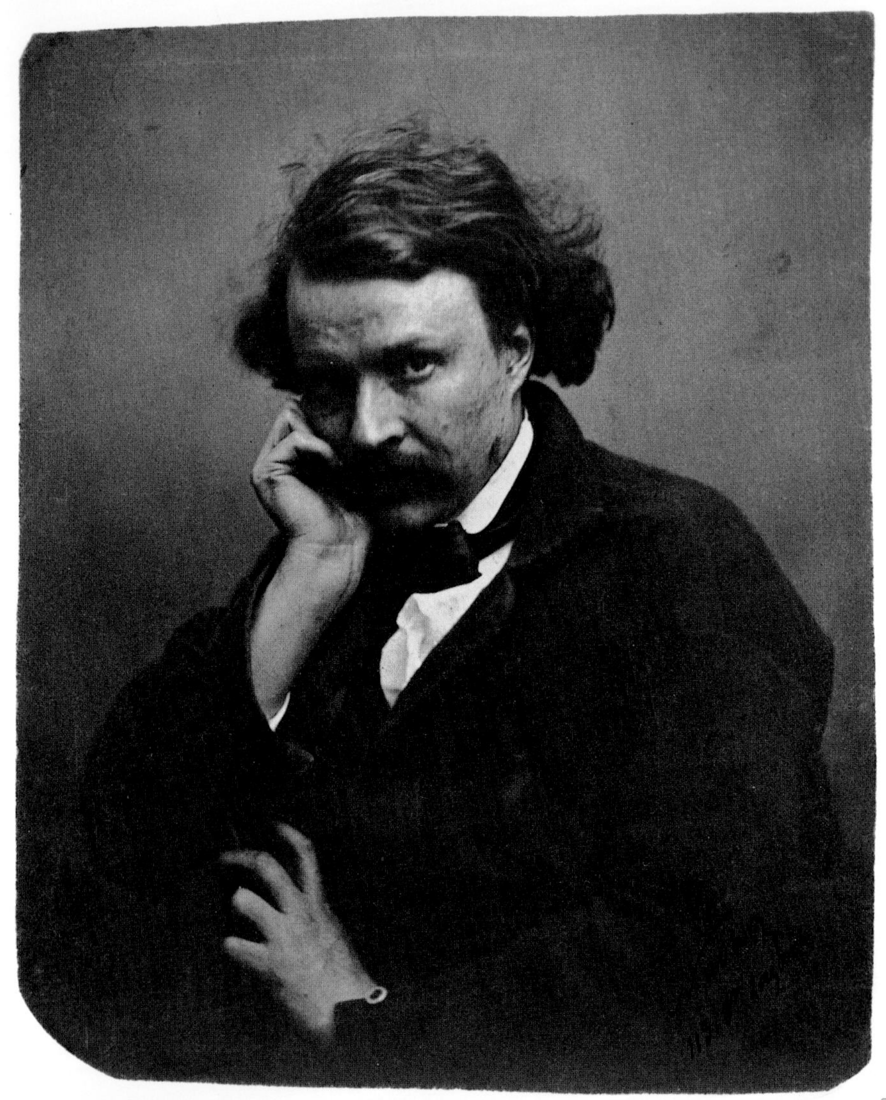

2.3

Gaspard-Félix Tournachon (1820–1910), nicknamed Nadar since boyhood, is often described as the first photographer to have raised the medium to the level of art. This achievement was facilitated by a background that made Nadar far more than simply a photographer. Student of medicine, caricaturist, journalist-critic, novelist (*La Robe de Déjanire*, 1845) and left-wing adventurer – as well as voluble friend to the most celebrated artists and writers of the Romantic and Realist periods – Nadar came to photography almost by accident. Having initially suggested it to his far less talented brother as a lucrative career, he soon took it up seriously himself. His approach was casual and spontaneous, personal and experimental – enhanced by considerable technical gifts honed in other media.

In 1856 Nadar summarized what he believed were the reasons for his success, which now constitutes a portrait photographer's artistic credo: 'The theory of photography can be learned in an hour and the elements of practising it in a day ... What cannot be learned is the sense of light, an artistic feeling for the effects of varying luminosity and combinations of it, the application of this or that effect to the features which confront the artist in you. What can be learned even less is the moral grasp of the subject – that instant understanding which puts you in touch with the model, helps you to sum him up, guides you to his habits, his ideas and his character and enables you to produce, not an indifferent reproduction, a matter of routine or accident such as any laboratory assistant could achieve, but a really convincing and sympathetic likeness, an intimate portrait.'

The photographer made these claims as part of a legal action aimed at preventing his younger brother Adrien Tournachon from using the name Nadar, which had become so famous that Victor Hugo once sent a letter addressed only to

'Nadar'. Adrien had been signing himself *Nadar jeune* (Nadar the younger), although no one had ever called him this. This was not simply a trademark dispute. More basic was the notion that an artist's work and therefore an artist's rights spring from individual talent, vision and even morality. However scientific and mechanical its process, photographic technology was merely a tool to be exploited by the man of genius.

In the winter of 1854, when Nadar first set up his own studio at his apartment at 113 rue Saint-Lazare, he was thirty-four years old, with a considerable career already behind him. The son of a print-shop proprietor who had recently moved to Paris from Lyon, Nadar was raised in a literate, politically leftist and libertarian environment. (His parents did not marry until 1826, a year after Adrien's birth.) In 1833 his father's business failed and three years later the family moved back to Lyon. There, according to his memoirs, Nadar began to study medicine, but the ensuing death of his father forced him to find remunerative work. He chose journalism, becoming a freelance theatre critic, in pursuit of which he returned to Paris with his mother and brother. He was a flamboyant character, tall and lanky with unruly red hair, bursting with energy and enthusiasm, though dressed shabbily and followed about by his droopy, emaciated dog. He was also an engaging conversationalist, if not a profound thinker. In his writings, as in his pre-photographic artistry, Nadar's witty *aperçus*, pointed barbs and devastating repartee held sway over consistent philosophy or sustained argument. His benevolent aims were always mixed with a hearty appetite for self-promotion and publicity. In *My Heart Laid Bare* (1869), Charles Baudelaire called him 'the most amazing expression of vitality'. Allied to Nadar's great charm were his loyalty and generosity, and his ready willingness to act even on far-fetched projects. In politics, his anti-authoritarian position drew the attention of the police, who reported on 15 June 1843 that he was 'one of those dangerous beings who spreads the most subversive doctrines in the Latin Quarter'. It is known that he would make unpleasant noises when passing a policeman. After his self-described political awakening during the 1848 Revolution, which overthrew King Louis-Philippe to establish a left-leaning republic, Nadar joined an expeditionary force for the liberation of Poland. As soon as they crossed the border into Germany, he and his comrades were promptly arrested. After some hard labour in a coal mine, he was back at the Café de l'Europe in Paris on 1 June, still wearing his fur-trimmed Polish hat. During the Second Empire, which he referred to as the 'Deuxième Tant-Pire' (the 'Second Much-Worse'), Nadar refused any public honours and attacked Napoleon III, whose *coup d'état* had overthrown the Second Republic, calling him 'Napoléon le Petit' (Napoleon the Small). Although he did not participate in the fighting of the Commune in 1871, Nadar openly visited friends in prison and hid a fugitive general in his home for two full weeks.

Nadar embarked on his career as a photographer at a time when two great movements in art and literature – Romanticism and Realism – were in full flower. Throughout the 1840s he belonged to the Parisian literary and artistic bohemia immortalized by his friend Henri Murger in *Scènes de la vie de Bohème* (1848). (Giacomo Puccini's famous opera *La Bohème*, 1896, is based on Murger's novel and the character of Marcel is said to be partly modelled on Nadar.) He also tried his hand with reasonable success – though not financial – at caricature, popularized by the advent of lithography and the spread of illustrated reviews. He worked closely with editors such as Jules Hetzel and Charles Philipon on satirical journals, among them *Le Corsaire-Satan*, *La Revue Comique* and *Le Journal pour Rire*. Among his friends were the leading lights of the younger generation: the poet and critic Baudelaire, the critic and storyteller Jules Champfleury, the renowned satirical lithographer Honoré Daumier, and the illustrators Gustave Doré and Constantin Guys. Among his acquaintances were established members of an older generation: the novelist George Sand (the pseudonym of Madame Aurore Dupin), the painter Eugène Delacroix, the composer Hector Berlioz, the poet Gérard de Nerval, the novelist and essayist Théophile Gautier. These led the way to other acquaintances, so that when Nadar began making celebrity portraits they were mostly those of long-term friends or others whom he either knew directly or indirectly.

Prior to taking up photography Nadar had already tried to capitalize on the representation of celebrities for money. He became a specialist in what was called the portrait-charge: caricatures of famous figures represented with oversized heads and tiny bodies. In 1854 he published his most ambitious project to date, the *Panthéon Nadar*, which, according to its advertising, assembled 249 'poets, novelists, publicists and journalists' in a procession of portrait-charges that wound its way back and forth across the wide, folio-sized sheet towards a bust of George Sand. The procession was led by Victor Hugo, Honoré de Balzac, and others ranked more or less as Nadar admired them. True to form, Nadar inserted himself at a strategic point, seated on a little mound near a sign on which he inscribed his flowery dedication. He planned separate sheets for theatre, visual arts and music, but never earned enough from the first plate to pay for them. Each figure was executed either from life or from a photograph. Nadar's idea for his brother's new profession may well have originated in this experience. In any case, it was shortly afterwards that Félix sent Adrien to Gustave Le Gray's photographic studio for lessons and then rented an atelier for him at number 11 on the fashionable boulevard des Capucines.

It was quite common for people to turn to photography following failure in other endeavours. As a new profession, it was wide open to newcomers, particularly immigrants. Early photographers had a sometimes unsavoury reputation, but it was a rapidly expanding profession. E. Ann McCauley traces the explosion of studios from thirteen in 1848 to approximately 365 in 1868. Of all of these, Nadar's is almost the only one to have survived in the general public consciousness of the history of photography. Nadar's notoriety within cultural and political circles gave a new twist to the image of the photographer. However, for him, recently married to Ernestine Lefèvre, photography was also a business that offered the opportunity for greater stability of employment and regular income.

Ernestine's dowry provided the capital to convert the ground-floor apartment on rue Saint-Lazare belonging to Nadar's mother into his first independent studio. He also built glass sitting rooms on his roof, accessed via one of the first elevators in Paris. Other investors ranged from the Jewish banking and railroad magnates Isaac and Émile Pereire, who had backed him as a caricaturist, to Nadar's former boss at the *Journal pour Rire*, Charles Philipon. Nadar's other journalist friends provided him with an extraordinary amount of news coverage and advertising, for which he only occasionally had to pay. *Le Figaro* of 22 July 1855 called him, 'the great Nadar, the true Nadar, the only Nadar, spiritual caricaturist, talented photographer, charming writer'. Between 1860 and 1861, after his initial success, Nadar undertook the extravagant renovation of a building at 35 boulevard des Capucines, in the heart of Paris's new commercial district. He constructed an iron and glass façade with a huge red facsimile of his signature splashed across it, lit by gas lamps at night. As a means of publicity, the move was a great success. Other high-profile stunts included banquets and costume balls, experiments with artificial light and exploits in aerial photography and ballooning.

The takeoff of photography as a profession in the early 1850s was directly linked to the invention of the collodion-on-glass negative (wet plate) process by Frederick Scott Archer in 1851. Until then, the dominant techniques were the daguerreotype, invented by Louis Daguerre in 1839, and the calotype. The latter used a paper negative and was invented by Henry Fox Talbot at about the same time, but never became very popular in France: the image was grainy and the paper negative was fragile. The daguerreotype process produced a highly detailed image etched directly onto a silver-plated surface, but it was slow, expensive and the unique image could not be reproduced. The new process, immediately and widely exploited in France, consisted of wiping a coating of wet collodion – made from cotton, ether and alcohol mixed with iodine – onto a glass plate, which would then be dipped into a solution of silver nitrate. Exposed to light before drying, this plate became a detailed negative that could be contact-printed onto an albumen- (egg white), salt- and silver-nitrate-coated paper, which was invented in 1852. (The dry plate collodion process was introduced in 1861.) The results were the fine, slightly purplish prints we associate with Nadar's early period. Adding to the expense of his work – his prices were among the highest in the field – was the fact that Nadar used large plates, approximately 19 x 25 cm. The first examples of such portraits were produced in 1854 in Adrien's studio, where Nadar had an interest in helping out in order to safeguard his investment. It is most likely that Nadar got his friends to sit for them and that he organized the poses and settings, while Adrien tended to the technical aspects. By the following year, Nadar had set up his own darkroom in his mother's apartment, using the courtyard as his naturally lit studio; by 1856 he was suing his brother for exclusive rights to the Nadar name.

Although Nadar concentrated on writers and other celebrities in the arts, rather than on the high and mighty in politics or business, his reception rooms were nonetheless sumptuously furnished in the latest cluttered fashion. By contrast, the studio itself – the outdoor courtyard where he took his exposures – was relatively spare. Nadar's concentration on faces was a crucial element of his successful style. He suppressed most props and insisted on neutral backgrounds, the use of dark costumes complementing his skilful lighting of the heads. His first work was often done in full sun, with the sitter placed so that one side of the face was more brightly illuminated than the other. That contrast led to what some have called Nadar's 'Rembrandtesque' effects. Most portraitists represented their sitters in street dress or formal attire in order to display their station in life; Nadar's approach was just the opposite. The clothing he draped around his models tended to generalize their presence rather than fix them in contemporary time. The heavy coats in which he posed figures like the Socialist politician Jean Journet (page 67) or the poet Charles Baudelaire (pages 31 and 33) muffled the details of the body and hid the hands, with the result of heightening the body's monumentality. Berlioz (page 49), whose head was notoriously large, seems well proportioned and imposing in Nadar's photograph.

Such use of costume has often been compared to the draperies in Baroque portraits, like those of Anthony Van Dyck, to whom the early critic and supporter of photography Francis Wey recommended that photographers should look for example. However, unlike the flashy reflections and complex folds often found in the Baroque style, the bulk and simplicity of Nadar's draperies recall the more sculptural works of Renaissance painters such as Masaccio or Fra Bartolommeo. Indeed, Nadar's portrait sitters often seem endowed with that *gravitas* so characteristic of the classical. Critic Shelley Rice has pointed out that Nadar's mixture of the ephemeral and the eternal typifies modern ambivalence towards progress. Nadar's technology was the most current, but his aesthetic aims were transcendent.

Nadar's strategies came directly out of his work as a caricaturist, which he continued to practise alongside photography until Philipon's death in 1862. Caricature was in turn related to the much broader cultural tradition of character study. Since the *Physiognomical Fragments* (1775–1802) by Johann Kasper Lavater, it was generally believed that character could be determined scientifically from close observation of facial and cranial features – a medical science called phrenology. A study of facial expressions was one of the early enterprises of the first studio, on which Nadar and Adrien collaborated. Undoubtedly through Félix, who had briefly studied medicine, Dr Guillaume Duchenne commissioned a series of photographs in 1854 to illustrate his treatise *Mécanisme de la physionomie humaine* (published in 1862), which was based on applying electrical currents to various spots on the head. A concept related to the study of physiognomy was the practice of social typing – portraying different professions and classes through representations of faces, postures, gestures and costumes considered typical. Vast collections of such imagery proliferated, as in the serial publication *Les Français peints par eux-mêmes* (*The French Painted by Themselves*, 1839–42), which was subtitled 'a moral encyclopedia of the nineteenth century'. Nadar was also a great admirer of the novelist Balzac, who claimed his collection of stories and characters *The Human*

Comedy surveyed the full range of human situations and emotions in the contemporary world. Picking up from Balzac in the 1860s, the Naturalist writer Émile Zola compared his own studies of human passions in different situations to medical forensics. This quasi-scientific interest in observing reality was, Zola noted, the dominant philosophy of the age. And what better instrument of panoptical observation than photography?

With his background in theatre, Nadar also had a deep interest in mime. He was close friends with the famous mime artist Baptiste Deburau and his son Jean-Charles, for both of whom he wrote plays. Deburau was a guest at Nadar's parties, and Jean-Charles posed for an extraordinary series of photographs (1854–5), in which he is dressed as the *commedia dell'arte* character Pierrot in order to help publicize the struggling studio. Françoise Heilbrun has persuasively argued that Nadar himself must have participated extensively in the arrangement and lighting of these images, even though Adrien probably shot and printed them. Their very conception goes to the heart of Nadar's sensitivity and approach, as evidenced by one of the most famous of the series, *Pierrot Photographer* (page 21). Maria Morris Hambourg has astutely observed that Nadar's gregarious personality turned the entire process of posing, shooting, developing and printing into a performance, with the artist as the actor. She calls him a 'conversationalist artist', based on Nadar's account of how sessions at his studio were run. Apparently, the pace was leisurely, the informality enhanced by the fact that the studio at rue Saint-Lazare was also Nadar's home. Referring to one sitter, Adolphe Crémieux, a former Minister of Justice under the Second Republic, Nadar recounted: 'One sits down, one chats, one laughs, all while readying the lens; and when [he] is in place, well positioned and drawn out for the decisive moment, radiating all his natural benevolence, warmed by all the affection with which he feels himself surrounded', the shutter would be released. Assistants moved reflectors and props at the photographer's discreet command. Clearly he enjoyed the illusion of bonding with celebrities while theatrically exercising a sort of creative power over them.

Nadar's humour is revealed in a photograph of George Sand, taken around 1864, in which she has donned a Louis XIV wig that Nadar had worn to a costume ball. It is also present in a picture of Philipon holding a cigar (page 23), where his deformed shadow creates a caricature on the wall behind him. But one should not underestimate the element of narcissism in such strategies, through which Nadar called attention to his own performance as well as to his subject. On the other hand, great sensitivity can be seen in Nadar's soft-focus approach to Honoré Daumier (page 59), the nineteenth century's greatest caricaturist, with whom Nadar collaborated and whom he deeply admired. In the majority of the series of portraits that Nadar made of Daumier, one is drawn to his eyes rather than to other specific features of his face. Nadar thus emphasizes Daumier's vision and its analytic ramifications, as evidenced by his apparent thoughtfulness. They were the source of the artist's power (and his troubles with government censorship). No doubt Nadar felt both a sense of kinship and awe for this great sceptic's talent.

Nadar's style of portraiture fell well within the norms of nineteenth-century portraiture in other media, especially in its concentration on artists and celebrities. If it was understood that personality could be detected from the specifics of physiognomy, then the idealization practised in earlier times could hardly reveal the talent that was the basis of a sitter's fame. The Romantic conception of the great man was that the source of his achievement was internal, springing from innate gifts and imagination. Its mode of depiction therefore had to be realistic, in order to capture the external manifestations of those traits. It was expected by both painter and photographer that the sitter would reveal himself when properly coaxed. Thus the transition from art to photography was nowhere easier or more logical than in portraiture. Moreover, Nadar's Rembrandt-like lighting was frequently used by the Romantic portrait painters, appreciated for its ability to dramatize the figure against shadows, isolating it from time and place and intensifying emotion. Yet Rembrandt was also associated with Realism – for his pitiless scrutiny of the marks left by age and experience on the human face. Even the notorious Realist painter Courbet's portraits were overtly Rembrandtesque in this sense.

Nadar's invitations to celebrities to sit for him at reduced prices were aimed at accumulating a collection of portraits that could then be publicly sold. This notion of collecting and selling celebrity portraits was already inherent in his lithographic venture, *Panthéon Nadar*. Unlike today's multiplication of images of public personalities through various news media, in the mid-nineteenth century celebrity was a matter of name rather than of visual record. Photography would change that, with Nadar's help. His portraits satisfied the natural curiosity that wishes to put a face to a name. They also played to the desire of many to associate with cultural leaders by displaying images of them in their personal surroundings. Foremost among those associated with such figures was Nadar himself, who could enjoy the paradox of earning a living while perpetuating his reputation as a member of literary bohemia. Nadar kept his negatives and made prints to order. It was the success of this enterprise that raised him to the greatest fame and led him to open the huge studio at 35 boulevard des Capucines.

The different periods that can be detected in Nadar's work are defined largely according to the change in studio and processes. In the new studio, Nadar added a few more conventional props, such as the half column in his portrait of Sarah Bernhardt (page 107), and the velvet chair with long tassels in the portrait of Édouard Manet (page 103). Ironically, at the very time he was preparing the new space, Nadar's brand of portraiture was encountering stiff competition from a new type. This was the smaller carte-de-visite photograph, invented and popularized by A. A. E. Disdéri, who took out a patent for it in 1854. By the early 1860s these four-inch long, pocket-sized, mass-produced photographs had become the rage, eminently collectible at a fraction of the price of the standard studio photograph. Disdéri had succeeded in getting the Imperial family to pose for him, and from that moment on, the fad was launched. Nadar conceded to the carte-de-visite by rephotographing his full-size prints in a smaller format – with a consequent loss of visual quality. In order to keep up with his debts and resist competition, he was also forced to conduct business along more efficient commercial lines – with a consequent loss of the interest it held for him. In the early 1860s he photographed numerous celebrities in a smaller format, stockpiling negatives on which he could draw in the future. He then left the shop primarily to assistants while he pursued other interests, except when subjects such as the famous young starlet Sarah Bernhardt came to pose. Among Nadar's friends, word quickly spread that he had lost interest in taking the portraits himself, preferring newer ventures.

Compensating for Nadar's short attention span were his enormous curiosity and inventiveness. Already in the late 1850s he was experimenting with artificial light, as in a wonderful self-portrait (page 87), whose purpose was publicity as much as science. He made a group of studies of a hermaphrodite (page 91), with medicine once again in mind. Taking his batteries and lights, he made photographic visits to the underground Paris of the Catacombs (page 93) and its modern sewers (page 95). And as part of a new obsession with ballooning (he dubbed his huge balloon 'Le Géant') and heavier-than-air flight, he photographed the city from above (page 117).

Although these late works are hardly aesthetic masterpieces, they expanded the frontiers of photography. All the while, competition was battering the portrait enterprise, and Nadar finally abandoned his boulevard des Capucines studio for more modest quarters in 1872. He also conceded daily management of the business to his wife and son Paul. From then on, Nadar withdrew to a semi-retired and self-absorbed state, during which he renewed his literary efforts. He concentrated especially on his memoirs, which would maintain his legend as the man who made photography into art. Just as photographs had frozen reality in time, Nadar would attempt to preserve his image of everlasting youth and fame through words.

Adrien Tournachon, Paris, 1854–5. Adrien Tournachon (1825–1903) was Nadar's younger brother, whom he had set up in the photography business. This portrait, one of a series, is among the early experiments on which the two collaborated. With his straw hat and cigarette, Adrien adopts the pose of the bohemian, whose casual attire and unconventional manner convey the independence associated with artistic creativity.

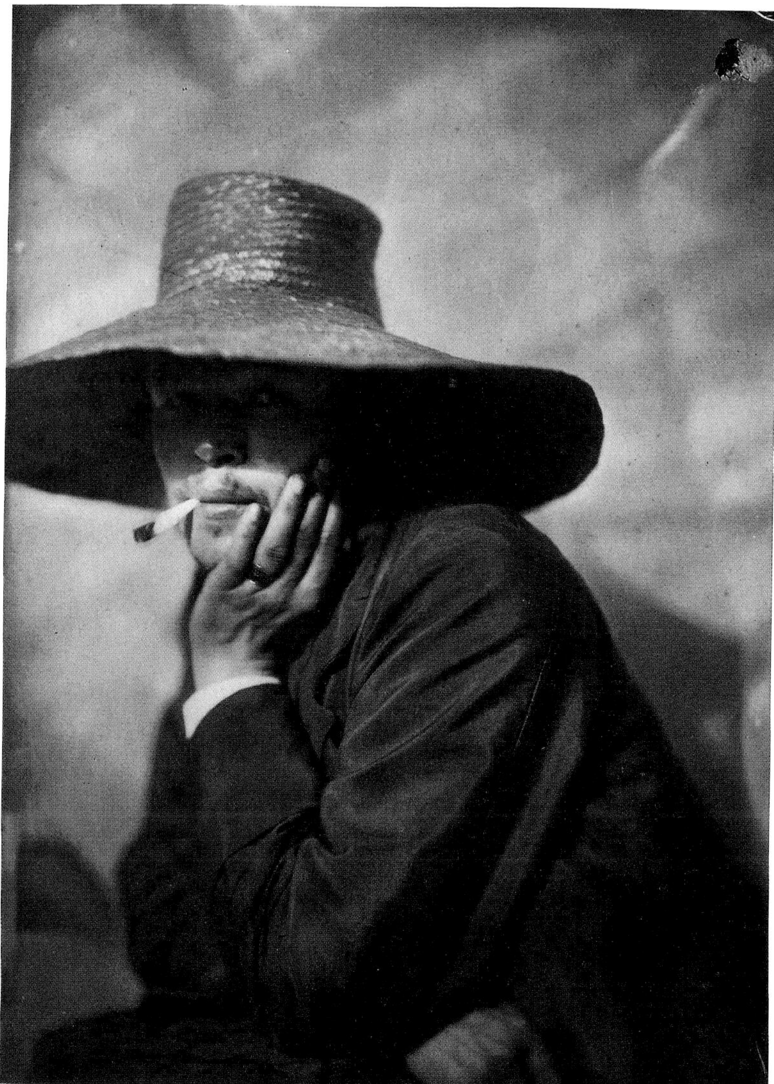

Pierrot Listening, Paris, 1854–5. With brother Adrien, Nadar produced a series of pictures of the famous mime Jean-Charles Deburau (1829–73), a close friend of Nadar from among his many theatre acquaintances. Deburau is dressed as Pierrot, the famous *commedia dell'arte* character. The series may have been intended to publicize the new business on which Nadar had embarked. Full-length portraits are rare in his oeuvre, as are explicitly theatrical poses, heightened here by the contrast of Deburau's white costume with the background.

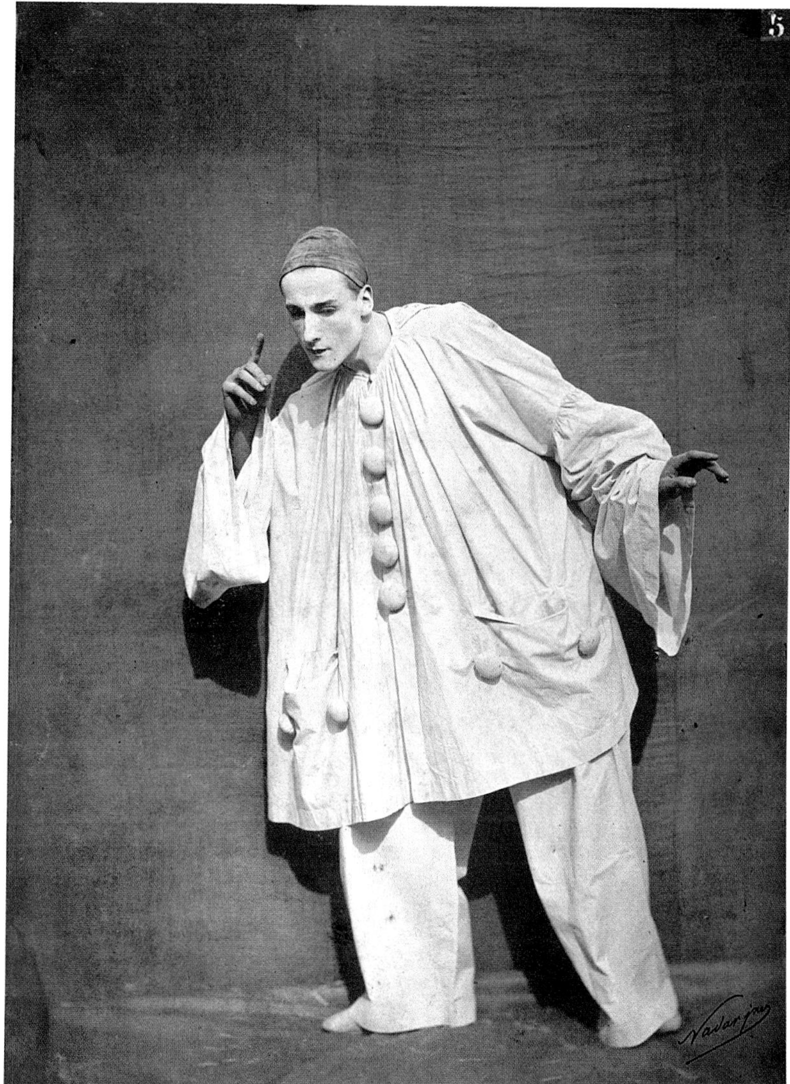
5

Pierrot Photographer, Paris, 1854–5. Of the series in which the mime Deburau posed for Nadar, this image is rightly the most famous, having to do explicitly with the art of photography. It seems to suggest that the posing session is a dialogue of performances between the photographer and his subject. In this composition, Nadar has used strong shadows to give the Pierrot costume an almost sculptural presence. In contrast to the extreme legibility of *Pierrot Listening* (page 19), here Deburau seems more natural in his thoughtfulness.

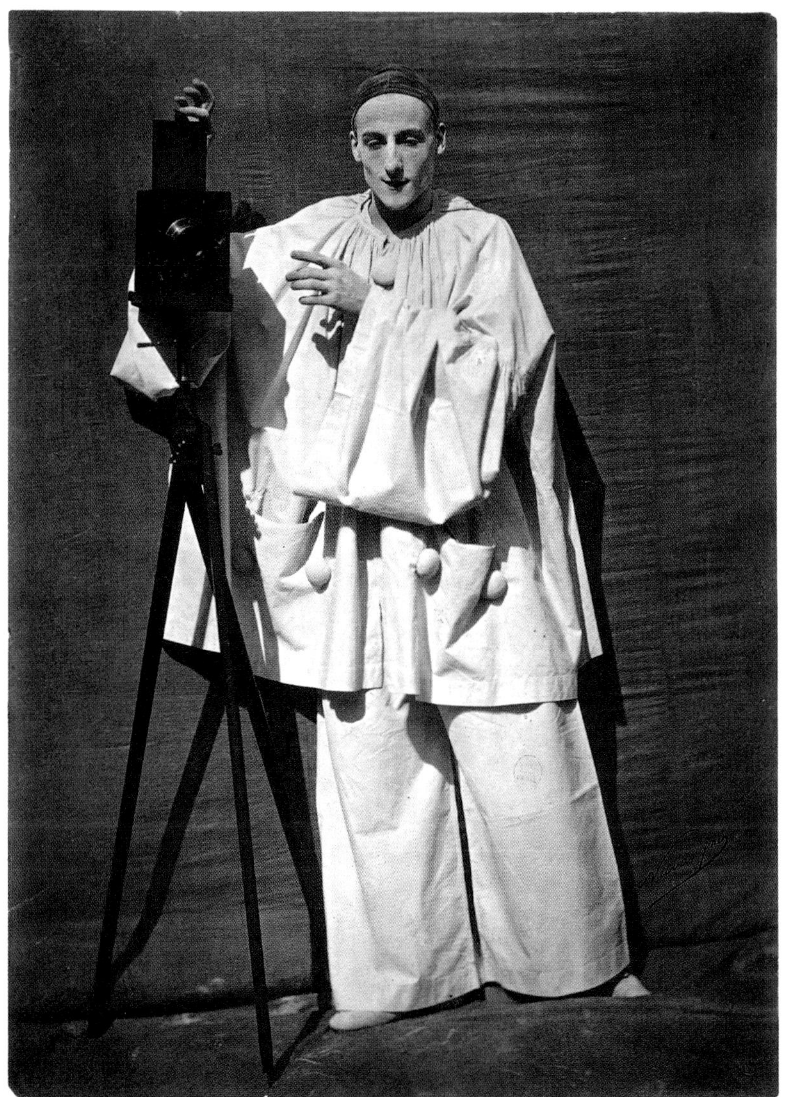

Charles Philipon, Paris, 1854. Charles Philipon (1800–62) was one of the fathers of political caricature in France, having founded the journals *La Caricature* and *Le Charivari* in 1831. Nadar's earliest portraits were of friends and associates like Philipon, Nadar's mentor, with whom he shared many of his liberal political beliefs. In a rare effect, he has used Philipon's shadow to create a caricature-like image in the background.

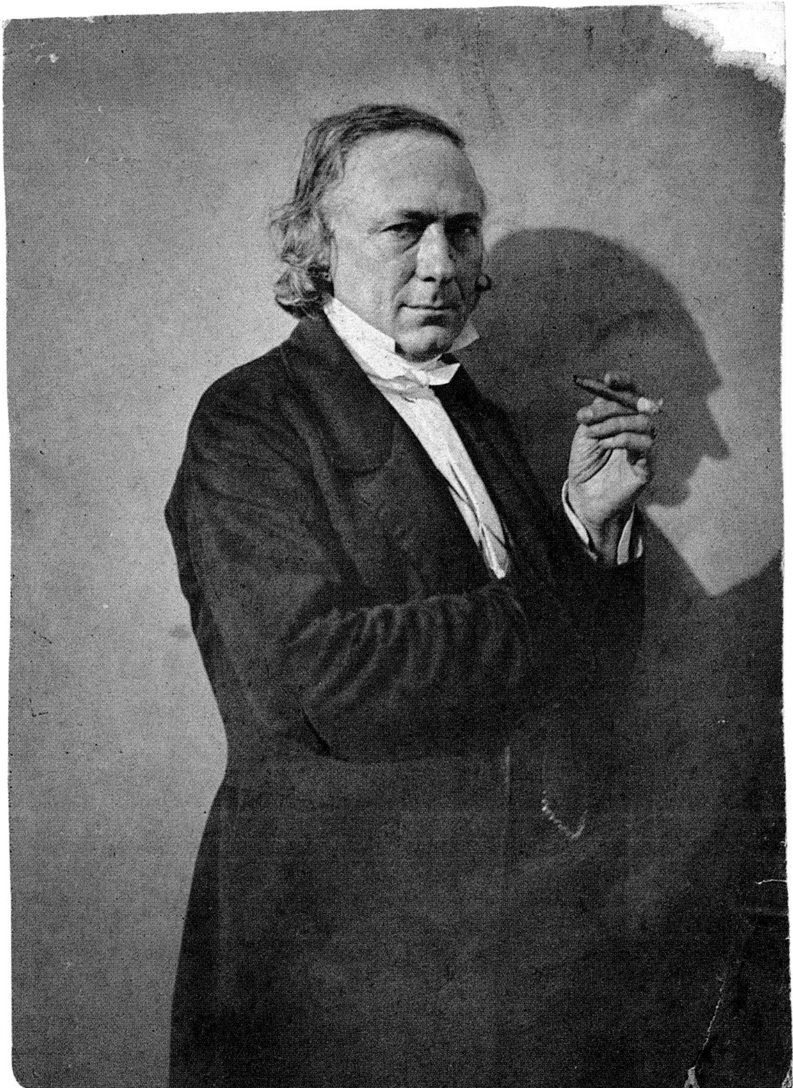

Gérard de Nerval, Paris, 1854–5. Gérard de Nerval (1808–55) was one of the leading Romantic poets of his day, much noted for his knowledge of German poetry, to which he helped introduce the French via his translation of Goethe's *Faust*. This portrait must have been made shortly before Nerval's suicide in January 1855. His rumpled clothing and grim expression suggest both his poetic unconventionality and the possibility of mental instability.

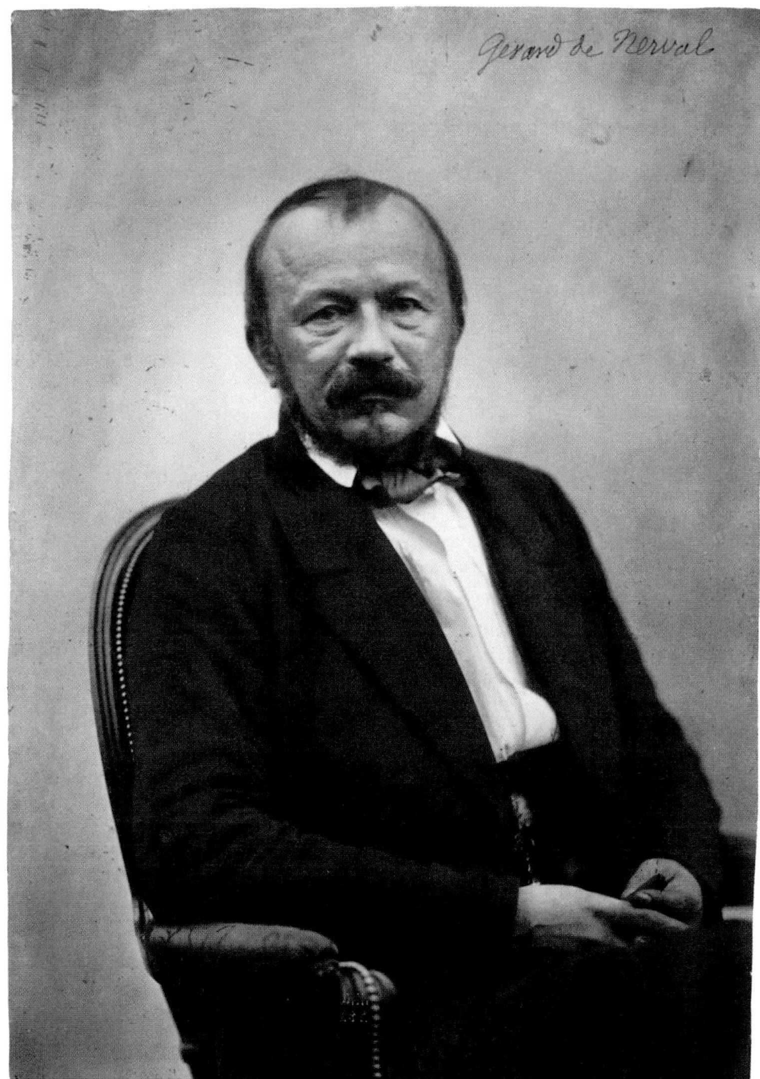
Gerard de Nerval

Théophile Gautier, Paris, 1854–5. The poet, novelist and critic Théophile Gautier (1811–72) was a leading champion of Romanticism. He initially trained as an artist, but his interest in the visual arts later took the form of criticism, noted for both its generosity and its volume. In 1856, after this photograph was made, he took over the editorship of the journal *L'Artiste*. The soft focus and the casual pose with open collar and rumpled coat suggest Gautier's intimate friendship with Nadar and his relaxed attitude towards conventional appearances.

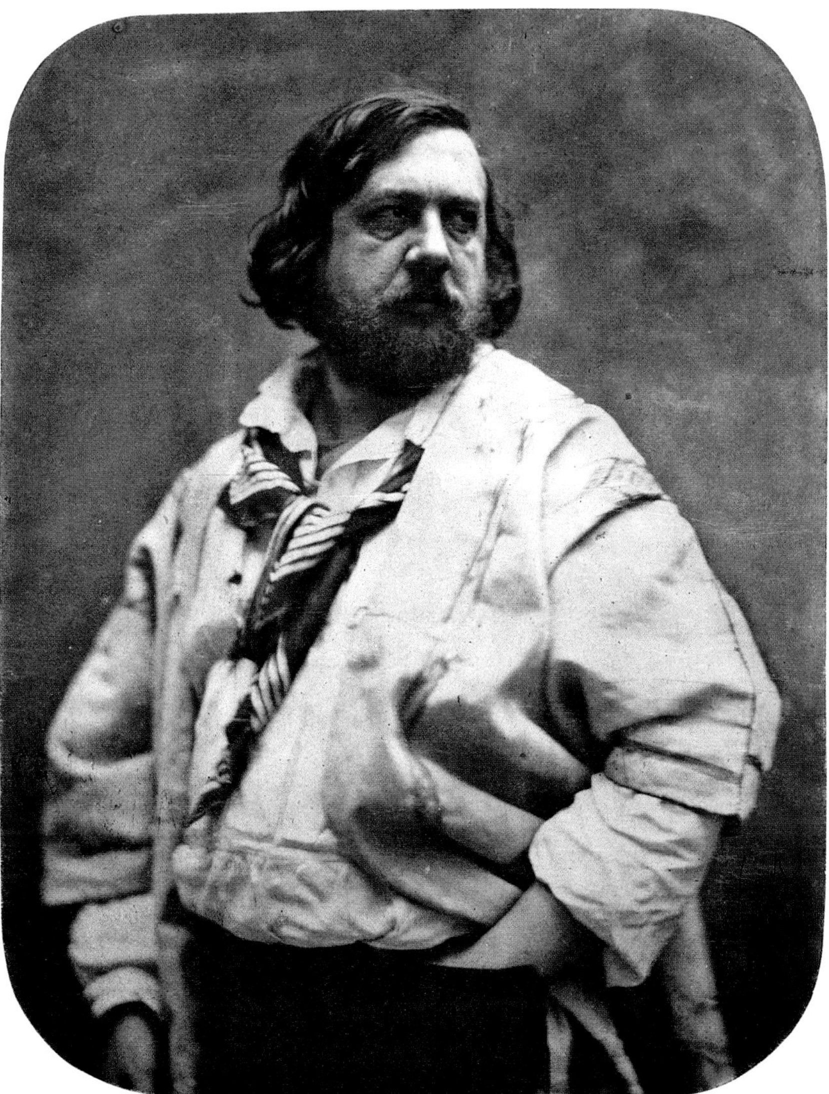

Auguste Préault, Paris, c.1854. Auguste Préault (1809–79) was a Romantic sculptor who defied academic conventions and loudly proclaimed his left-wing politics. With his arms crossed and shoulders hunched, he forms a tense, compact mass. His gaze upward and off to the side through squinting eyes implies the inner preoccupation of the artist-visionary. Popularized through painting, such poses were recognizable expressions of Romantic genius.

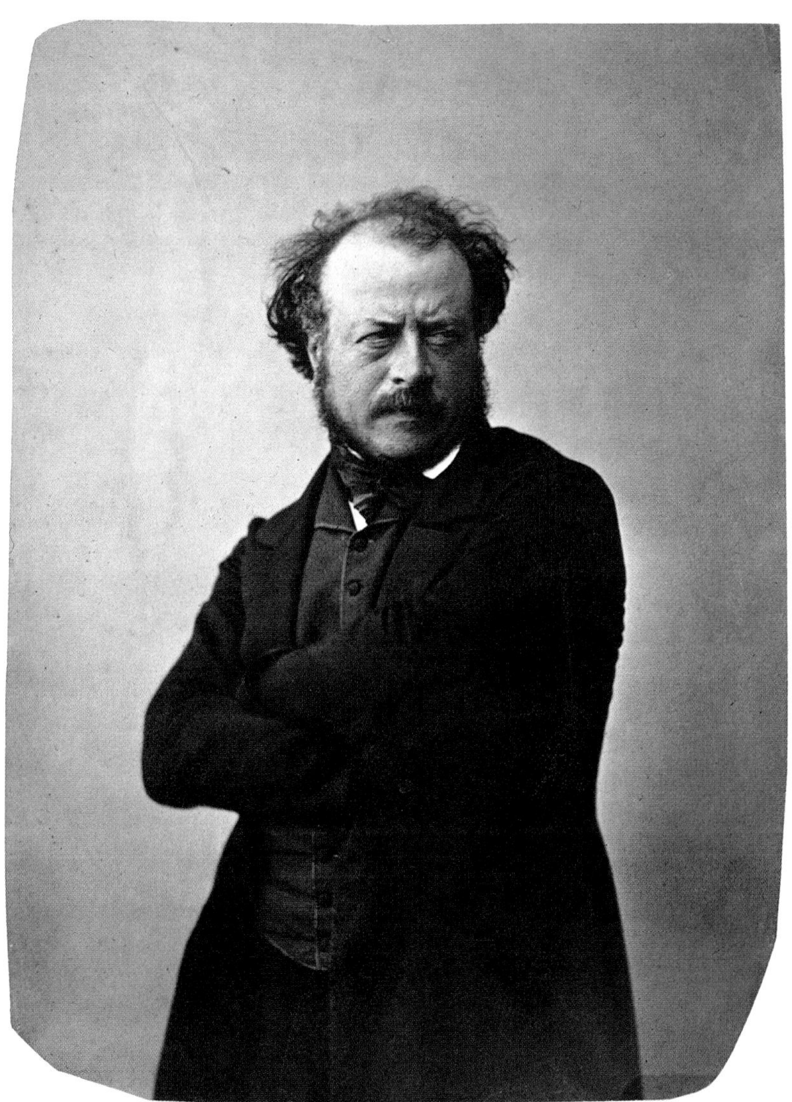

Charles Baudelaire, Paris, 1855. Charles Baudelaire (1821–67) was the most brilliant and notorious poet and critic of mid-nineteenth-century France. His collection of poems *Les Fleurs du mal* (1857) had created a scandal, and several were censored for offending public morality. Baudelaire was a close friend of Nadar, posing for several portraits. This image of the poet reclining in an armchair belonging to Nadar's mother, ostensibly lost in thought, is one of the earliest and most unconventional.

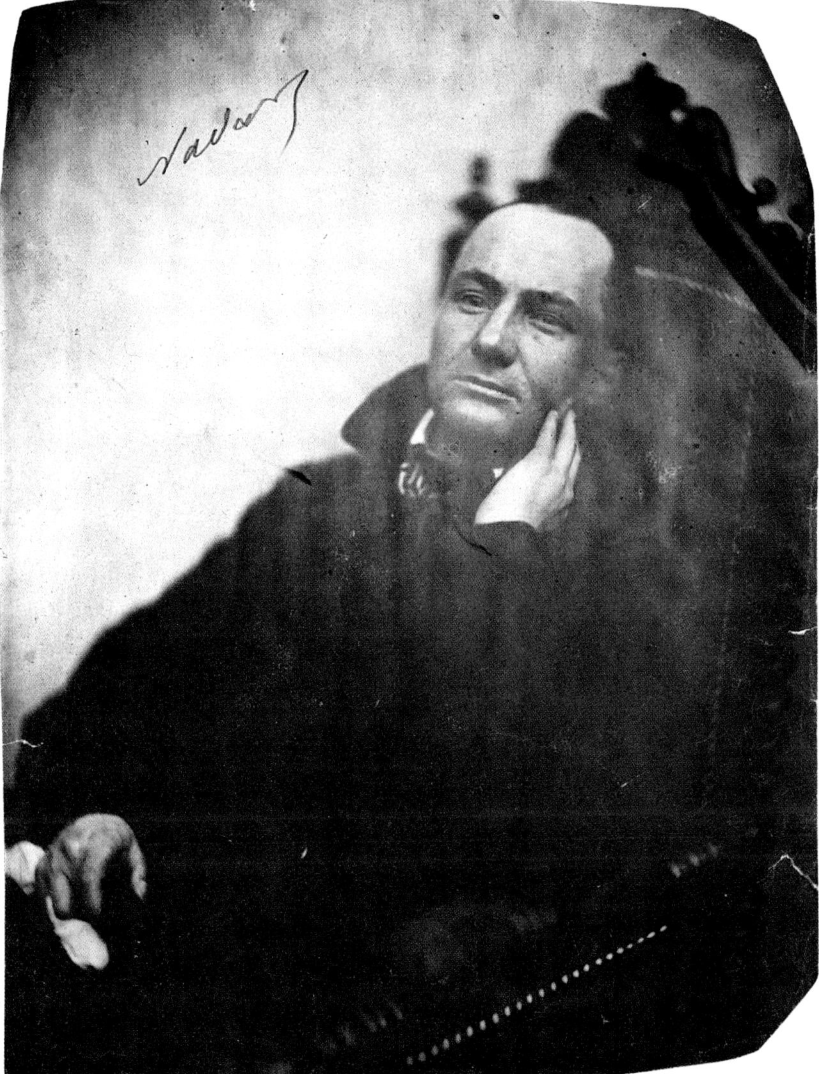
Nadar

Charles Baudelaire, Paris, 1855. This portrait of Baudelaire captures the intensity of the poet's glare. The bulky garment heightens the presence of his otherwise slim frame and sets off the refined features of his face. Other aspects of the pose achieve a balance between the classical (Baudelaire's right hand held inside his coat) and the informal (the left hand in his pocket). Baudelaire believed that photography would be the end of art, claiming it involved no exercise of imagination.

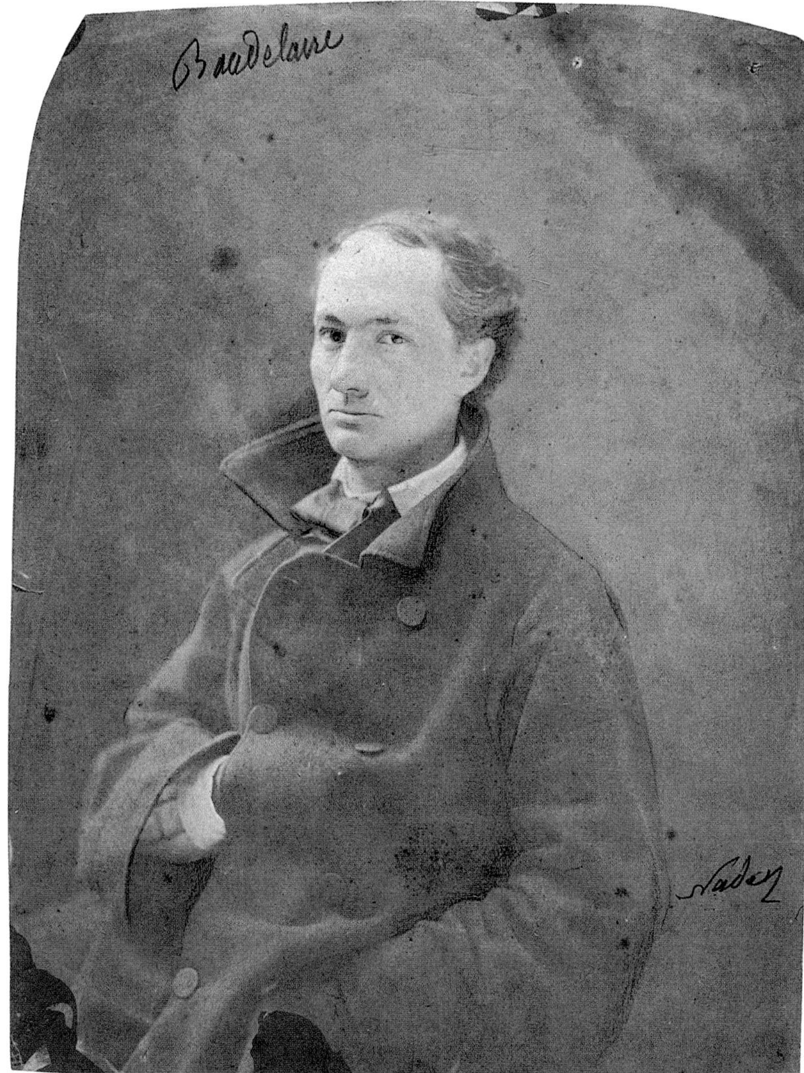
Baudelaire
Nadar

Alexandre Dumas père, Paris, c.1855. The novelist Alexandre Dumas (1802–70) was the son of a revolutionary general and a black mother. He had collaborated with Nadar on several theatrical projects. Largely self-educated, Dumas acquired fame as the author of historical novels, including *The Three Musketeers* (1844). Nadar's portrait presents him as self-assured and direct, flaunting the features and wavy hair that displayed his mixed origin. Straddling a chair backwards, Dumas seems filled with the vitality associated with his heroes.

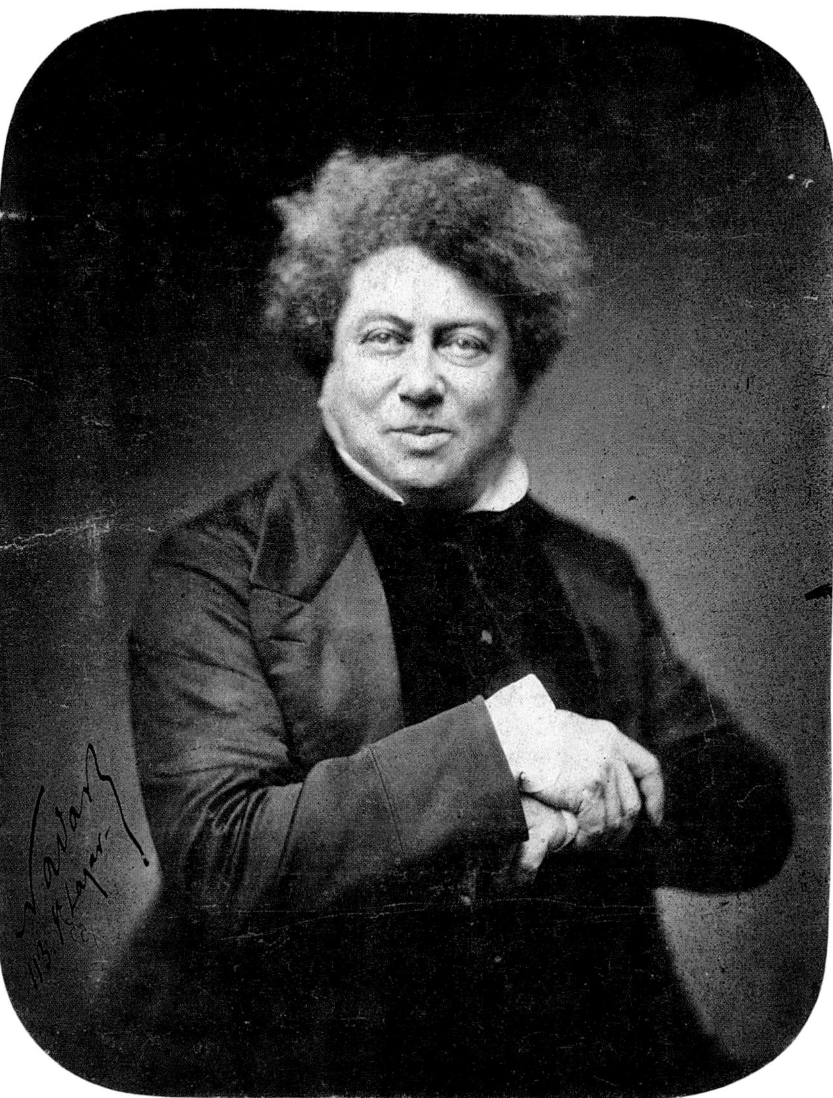
Nadar

François-Louis Lesueur, Paris, c.1855. François-Louis Lesueur (1820–76) was a famous comic actor renowned for the mobility of his facial expressions and for his wit. By 1855, Nadar had perfected simple but classical poses, using a wooden cut-off column as a prop. This portrait captures Lesueur's intelligent gaze; the beginnings of a smile may suggest a slightly mocking sense of humour.

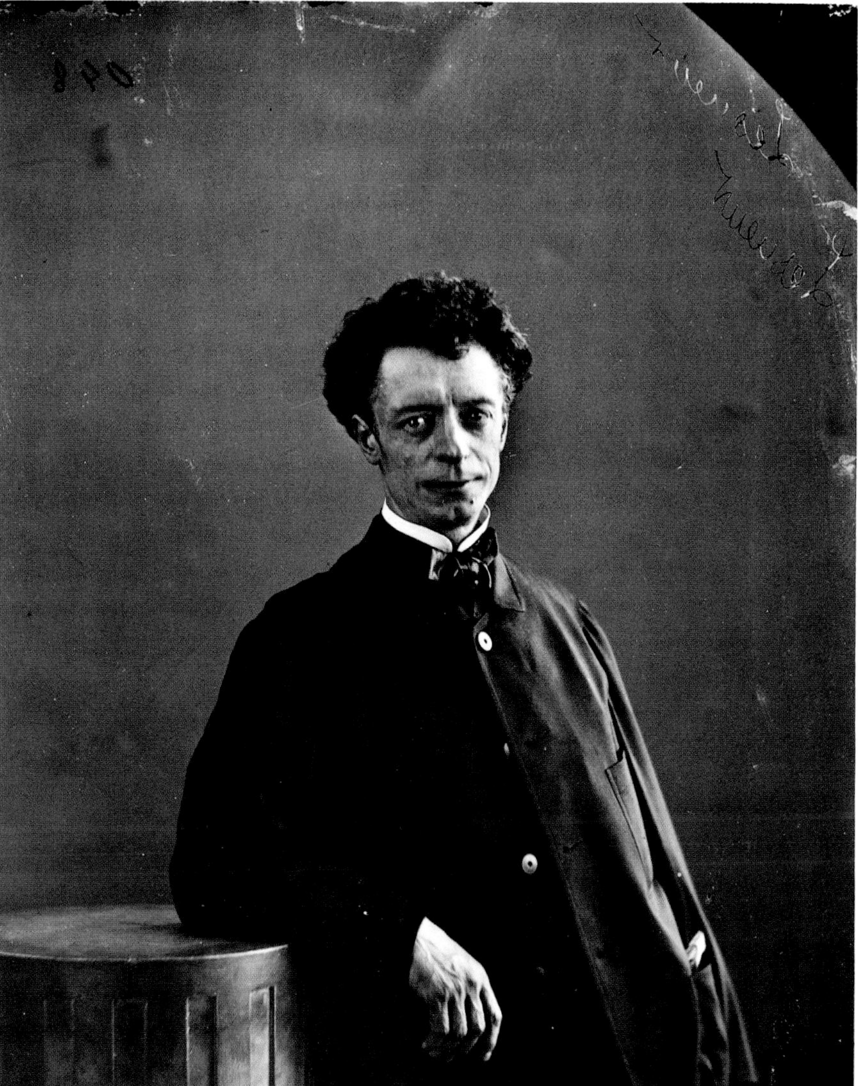

Edmond and Jules de Goncourt, Paris, c.1855. At the time of this portrait, the wealthy aristocratic brothers Edmond and Jules de Goncourt (1822–96 and 1830–70) had not yet attained the fame that their collaborations would bring them. Their diaries were remarkable for attention to detail and their novels treated what they regarded as the distasteful lives of ordinary people with brilliant literary artifice. This photograph is a study in contrast between the older Edmond (on the left), quiet and pensive, and his more extrovert brother.

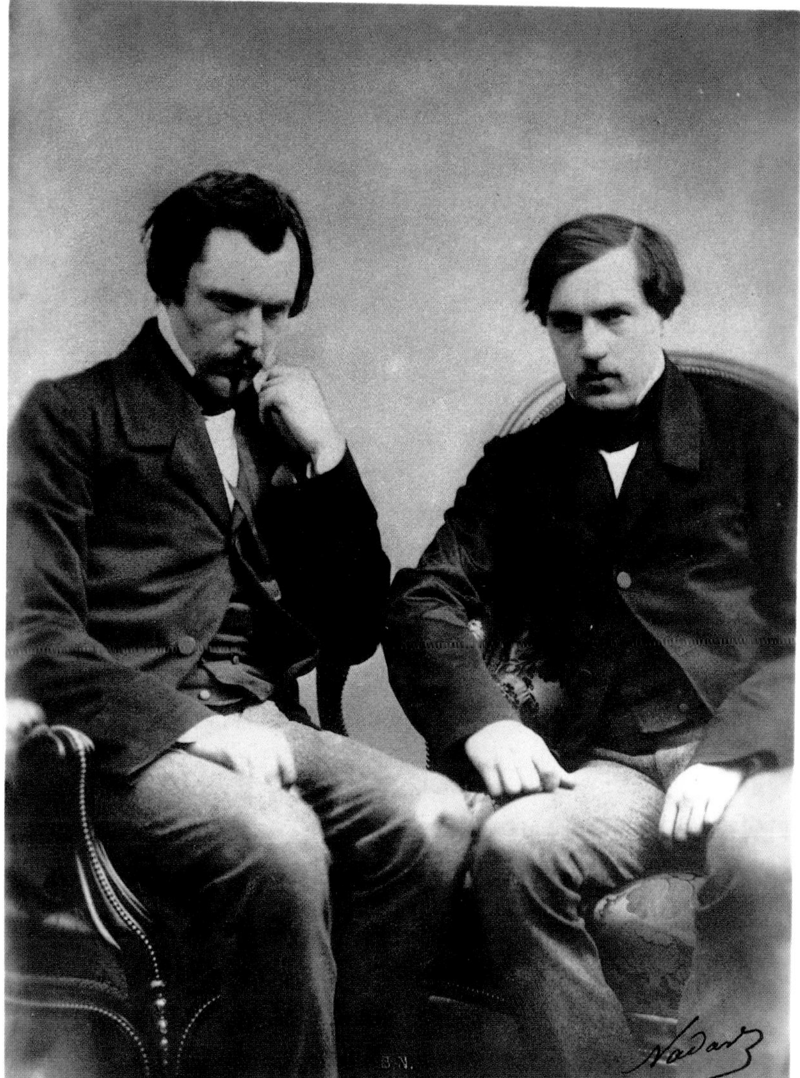
B.N.
Nadar

Standing Nude, Paris, c.1855. *Standing Nude* is a rare example of Nadar venturing outside the realm of portraiture in the early years of his photographic career. Yet in contemporary photography generally, the nude was a widely practised genre, fulfilling functions from the pornographic to an inexpensive substitute for artists' models. Nadar's aim seems to be primarily artistic, the *contrapposto* pose evoking classical statues and concentrating the eye on the decoratively spread draperies on the floor. That the model covers her face reveals the inconvenience of photographic realism: even the most ideal nude is still inevitably a portrait, possibly here of a girl known as Mariette, who may have inspired the Musette of Henri Murger's *Scènes de la vie de Bohème* (1848), on which Puccini's opera was based.

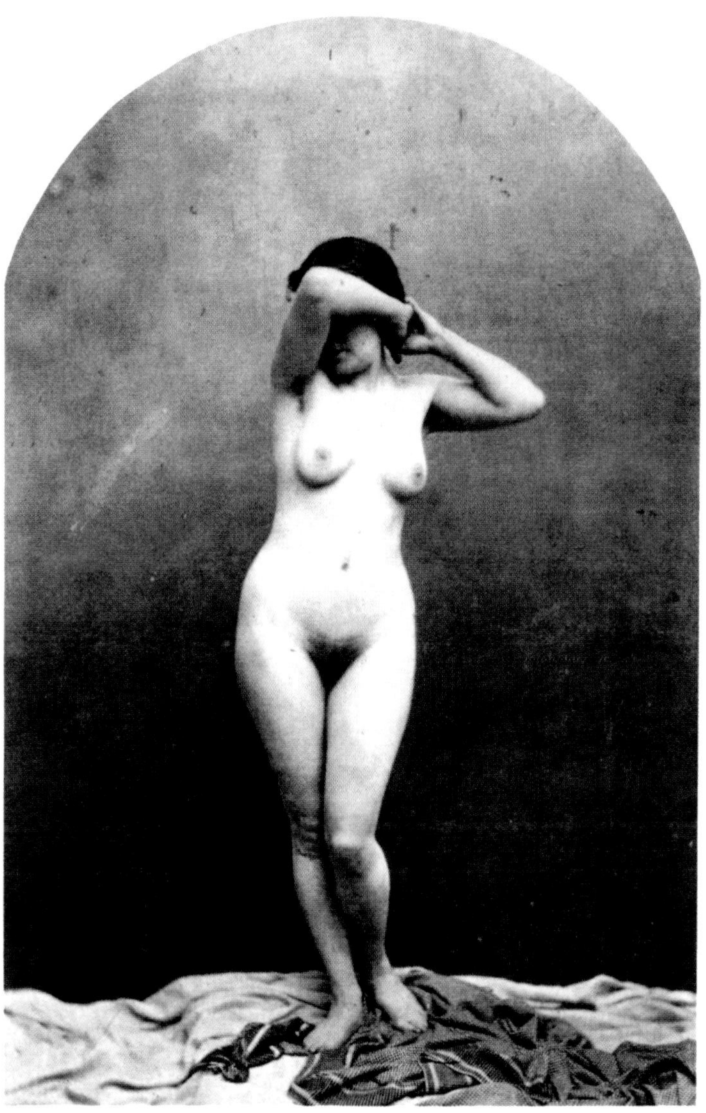

Jules Janin, Paris, c.1855. Jules Janin (1804–74) was a powerful theatre critic whose diverse, changing, inconsistent and sometimes unscrupulous opinions made him as many enemies as friends. His relationship with Nadar was intermittently warm and antagonistic. It has been claimed that this portrait of Janin's bloated form and disdainful expression reveals Nadar's abiding contempt and distrust.

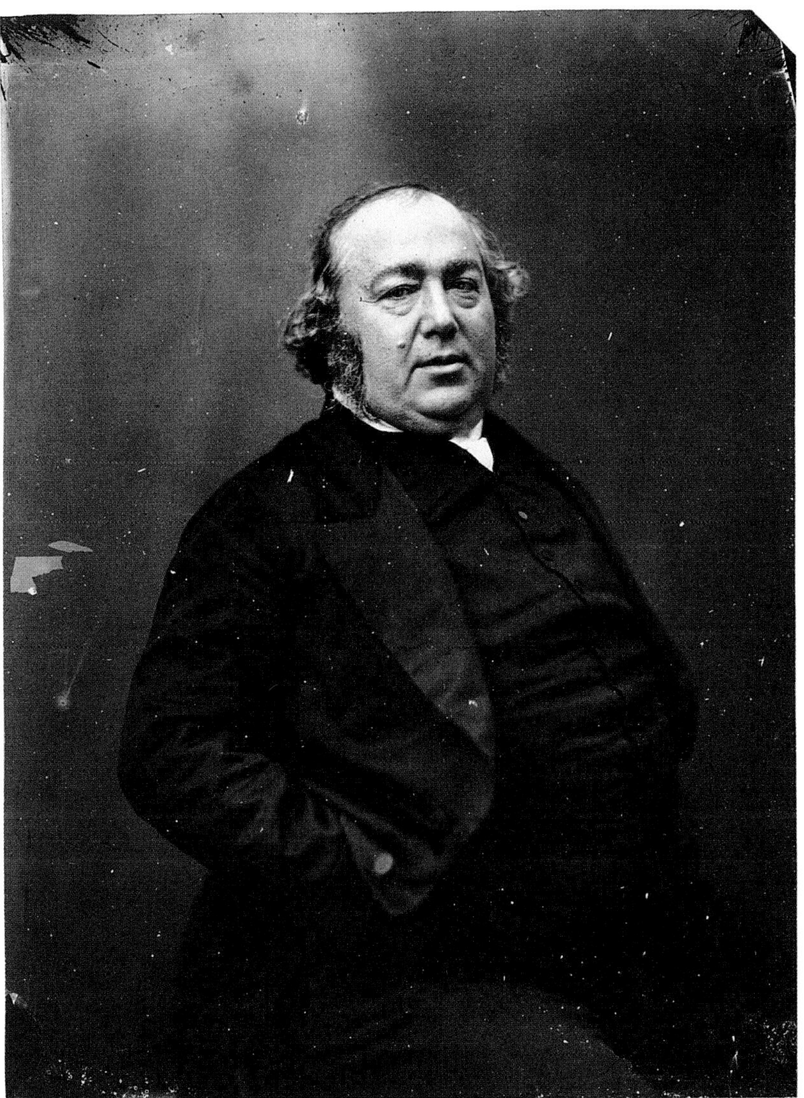

Kopp, Paris, 1855–8. Kopp (d.1872, first name unknown) grew up in an orphanage and had a varied career as a handyman, salesman, clown and itinerant actor before attaining some success in the comic role of insubordinate servant at the Théatre des Variétés. With his hair brushed up and dressed as a waiter in a café, Kopp adopts a similar role in Nadar's portrait.

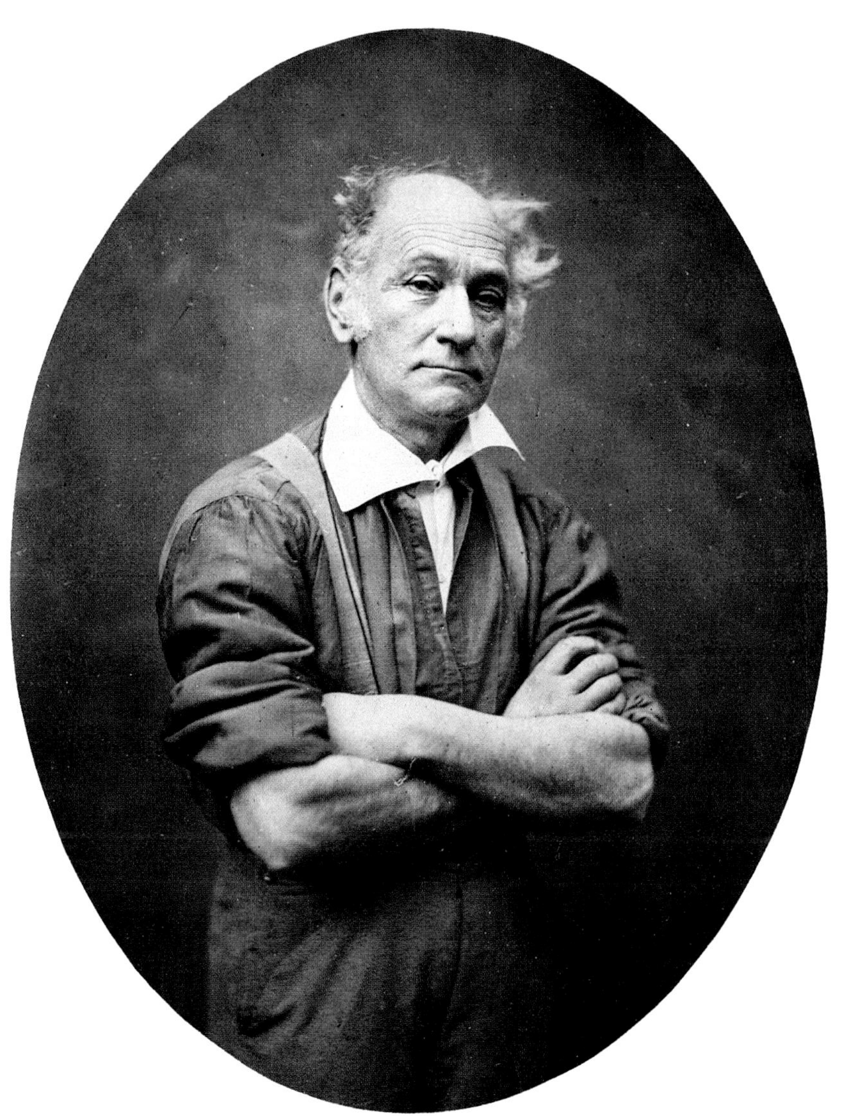

Marie Laurent, Paris, c.1856. Marie Laurent (1826–1904) was a renowned actress, but was not known for her physical beauty. Nadar's portrait from the back, trimmed to an oval shape, may represent a response to this reputation. Nevertheless, it creates a singular harmony from the waves of the actress's hair, the curve of her neck and shoulders, and the folds in her drapery. The result is an image of classical simplicity worthy of the great portrait painter Ingres.

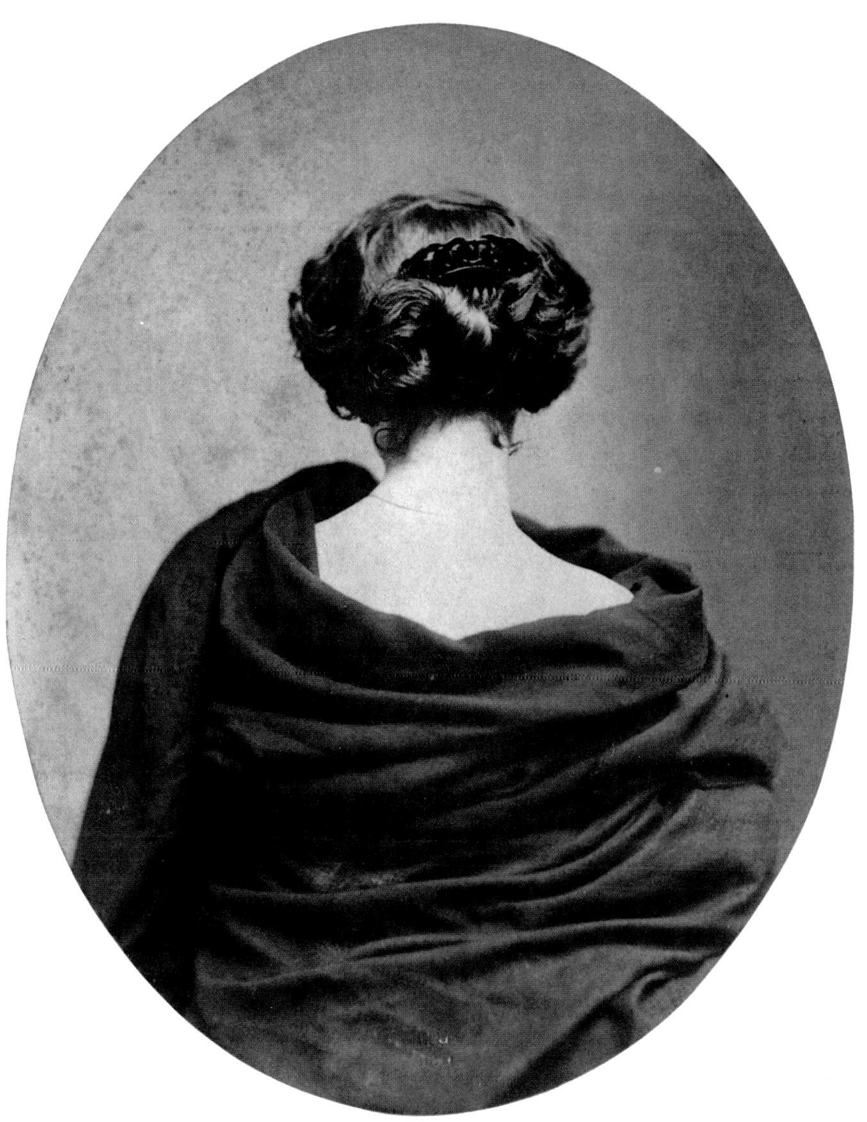

Hector Berlioz, Paris, 1856–7. Hector Berlioz (1803–69), the controversial Romantic composer and conductor, acquired fame with his *Symphonie fantastique* (1830) and *La Damnation de Faust* (1846), based on a translation by Gérard de Nerval (page 25). Nadar represents Berlioz with fierce dignity as a towering figure, whose monumental volume is enhanced by an oversized coat. The fixated gaze, prominent nose and ample head of hair contribute to the image of a Romantic visionary.

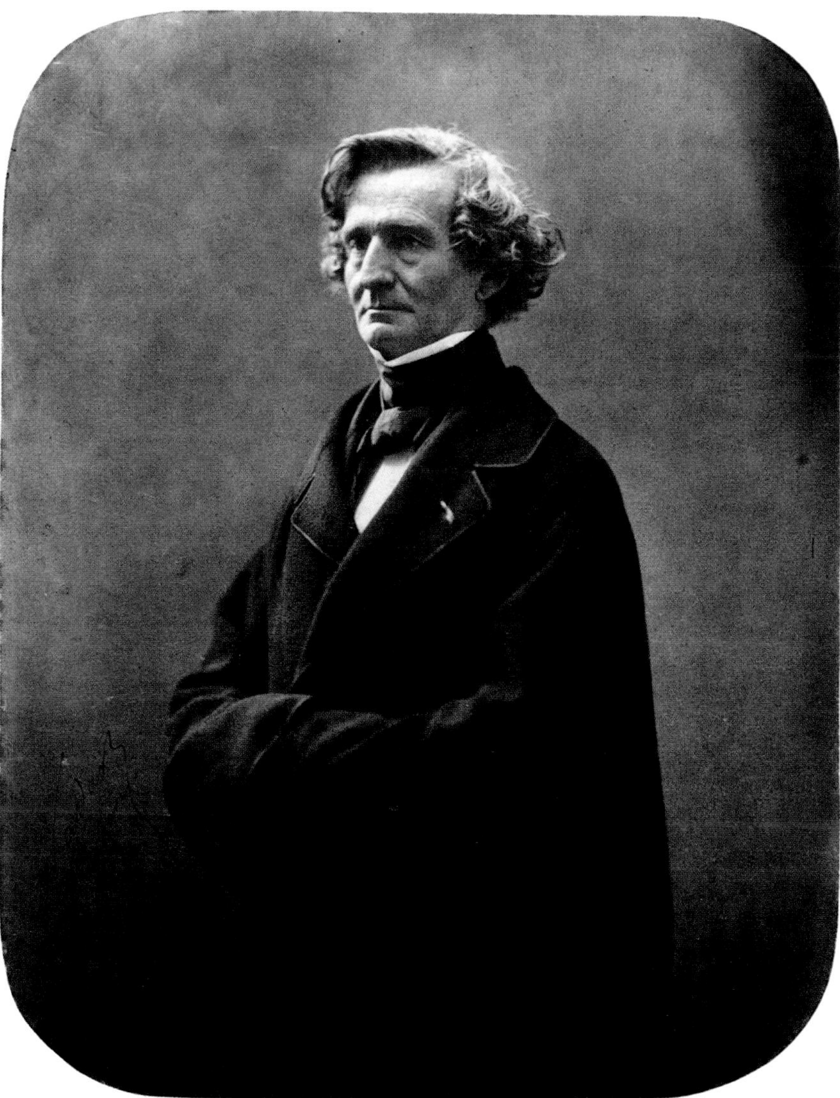

Paul Chenavard, Paris, 1856–8. Paul Chenavard (1807–95) was a painter of great intellectual and moral ambition whose utopian ideas were very much of their time and whose personality was popular in artistic circles. His work is practically forgotten today because of its allegorical complexity and classicizing, if not academic, style at a time of Realism and Impressionism. Nadar has cast the painter with crossed arms and has turned the head to create a meditative posture that, accompanied by the shadow, complements his melancholy expression. It is possible that Nadar implies both admiration for and yet a sense of the futility of Chenavard's ambitions.

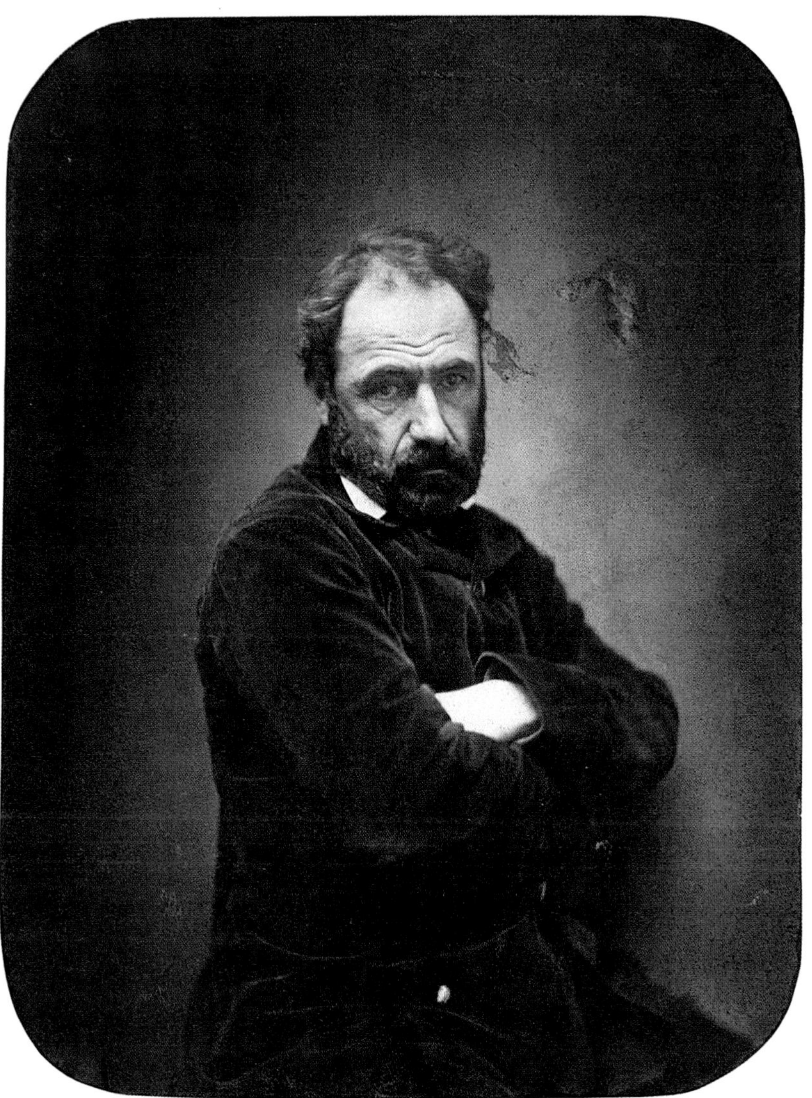

Rosine Stolz, Paris, 1856–8. Born in Spain, Rosine Stolz (1815–1903) rose from working-class origins to become an extraordinary diva, following her debut as Rachel in Halévy's *La Juive* (1835). She was known for both artistic and sexual excess. She was rumoured to have had affairs with the mime Deburau and with Baudelaire as well as lesbian relationships. In 1847, after being booed for a false note, she left France until 1854. Nadar shows the somewhat stern remainder of Stolz's fiery character, the latter evoked by her rich shawl and hair ribbons, at the end of her stage career.

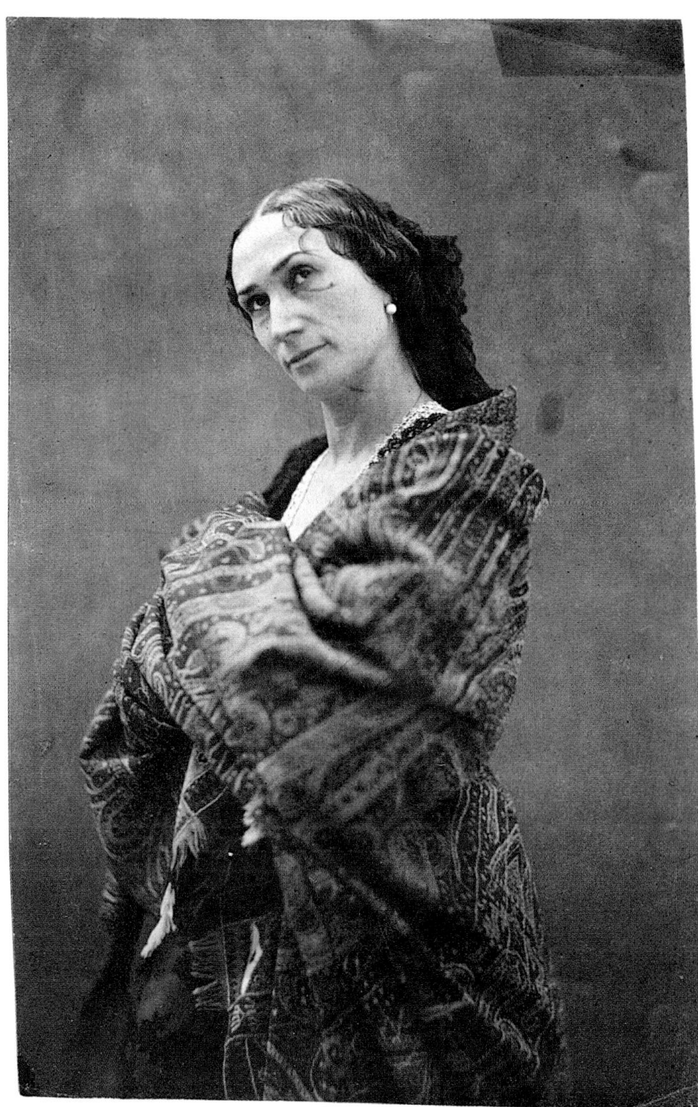

Pierre Cicéri, Paris, 1856–8. Pierre Cicéri (1782–1868) was the master of Parisian theatre décor, having given up a promising singing career because of an accident that left him with a limp. Although leaning on his cane, Cicéri is otherwise vigorous and alert, in a pose filled with spontaneous energy. With his eyes gazing off to the side and his unruly shock of white hair, contrasting with the darker background, he becomes an eccentric version of the Romantic artist.

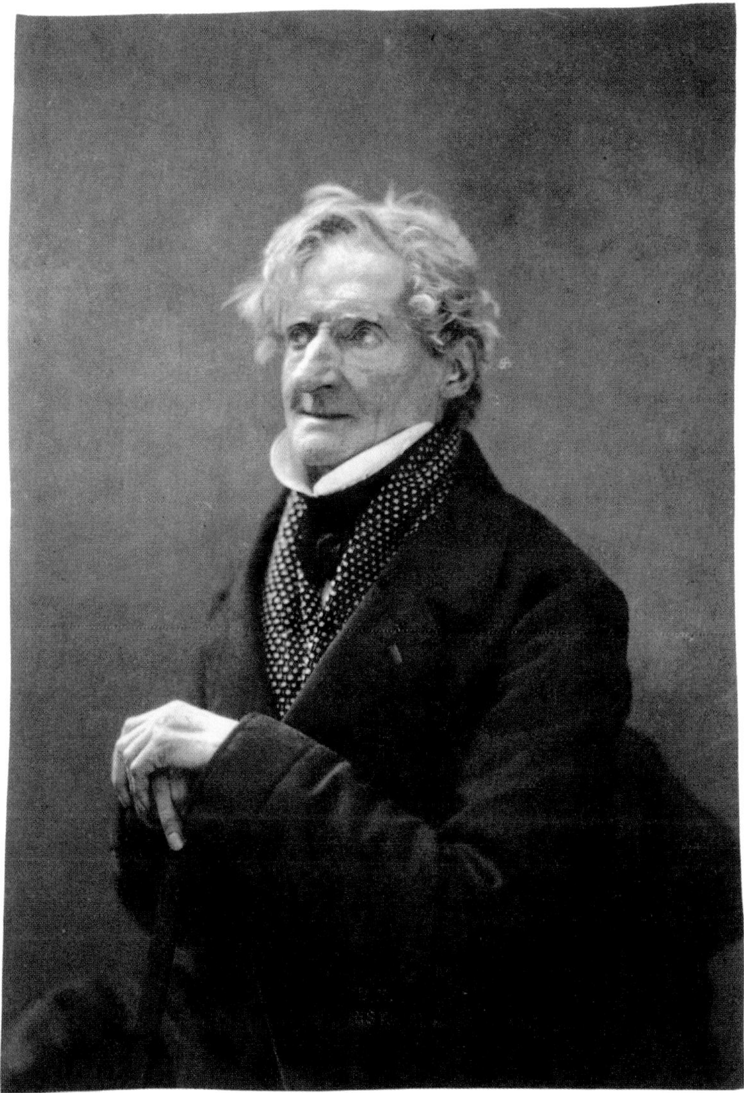

Jean-Baptiste-Camille Corot, Paris, 1856–8. Corot (1796–1875) was considered the foremost landscape painter of his day, combining elements of the classical tradition with the direct experience of nature, which he studied closely. He is represented here in his prime, perhaps a little self-satisfied, yet also hardy and rustic, reflecting his association with the rural painters of the Barbizon School. Corot's interest in photography led him to emulate certain effects such as blurring and soft focus in his later paintings. His teachings encouraged the study of nature at first hand and foreshadowed the work of the Impressionists.

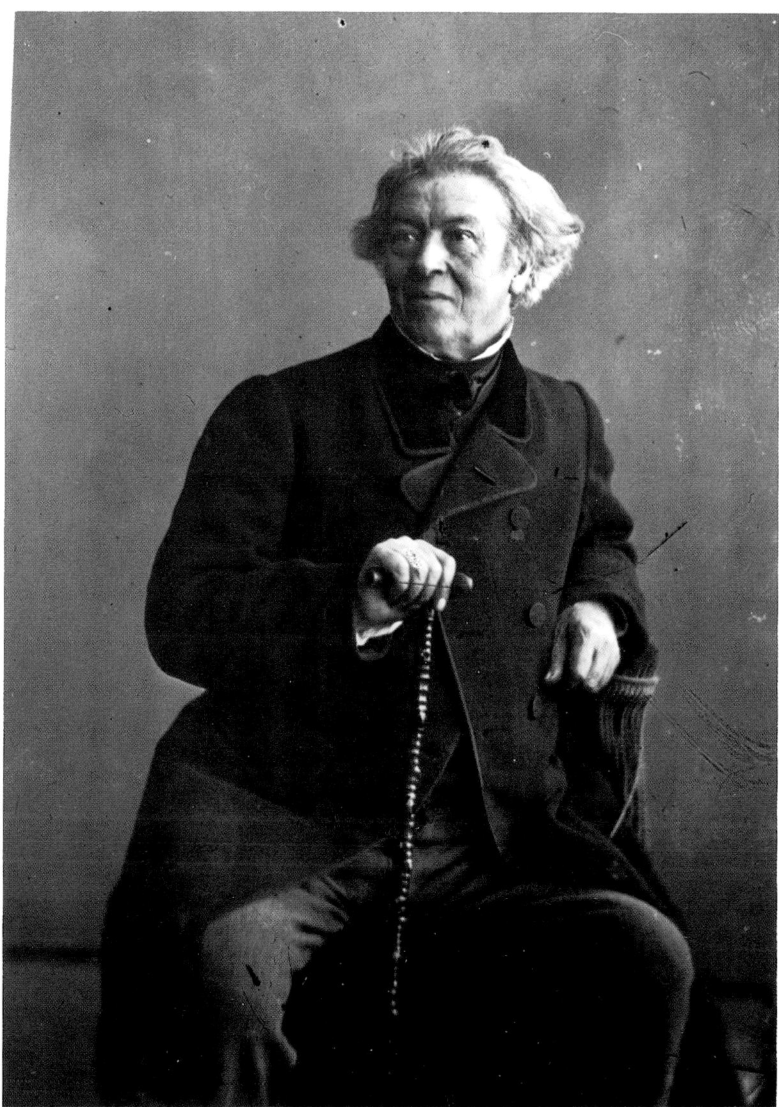

Honoré Daumier, Paris, 1856–8. Daumier (1808–79) was the most famous caricaturist in nineteenth-century France, known for his biting satires of political figures and other powerful members of society, as well as his more sympathetic chronicling of petit-bourgeois foibles and pretensions. He is considered one of the greatest draughtsmen of all time, with an eye capable of capturing the essence of forms in simple, summary sketches. In this portrait, Daumier's sideways glance and slightly turned head suggest that he has just noticed something worthy of his attention.

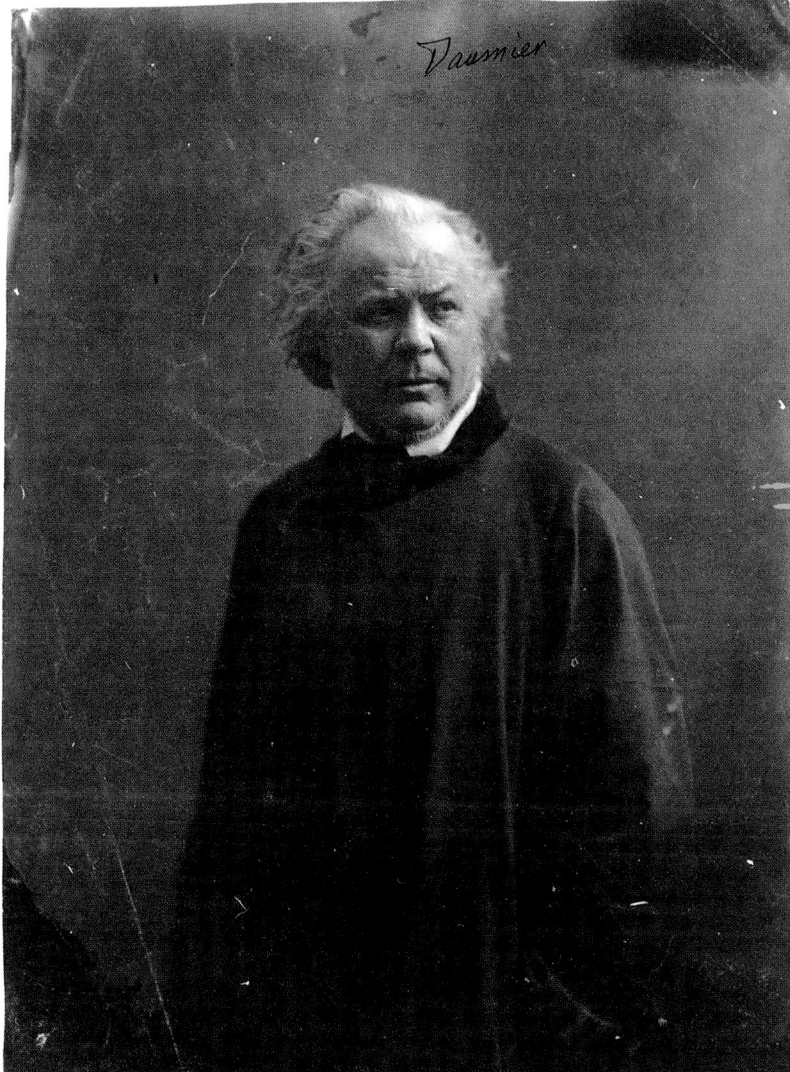
Daumier

Honoré Daumier, Paris, 1856–8. Another portrait of Daumier – Nadar made four at the same sitting – is a rare profile view. Here, the lithographer clearly seems to be observing some thing or activity outside the picture frame, his eyebrows slightly furrowed as he sharpens his attention in the direction indicated by his pointed nose. The considerable bulk of Daumier's body enhances our sense that he is artistic master of the situation, which he will capture with the same kind of easy, rapid gesture he has used to comb his hair.

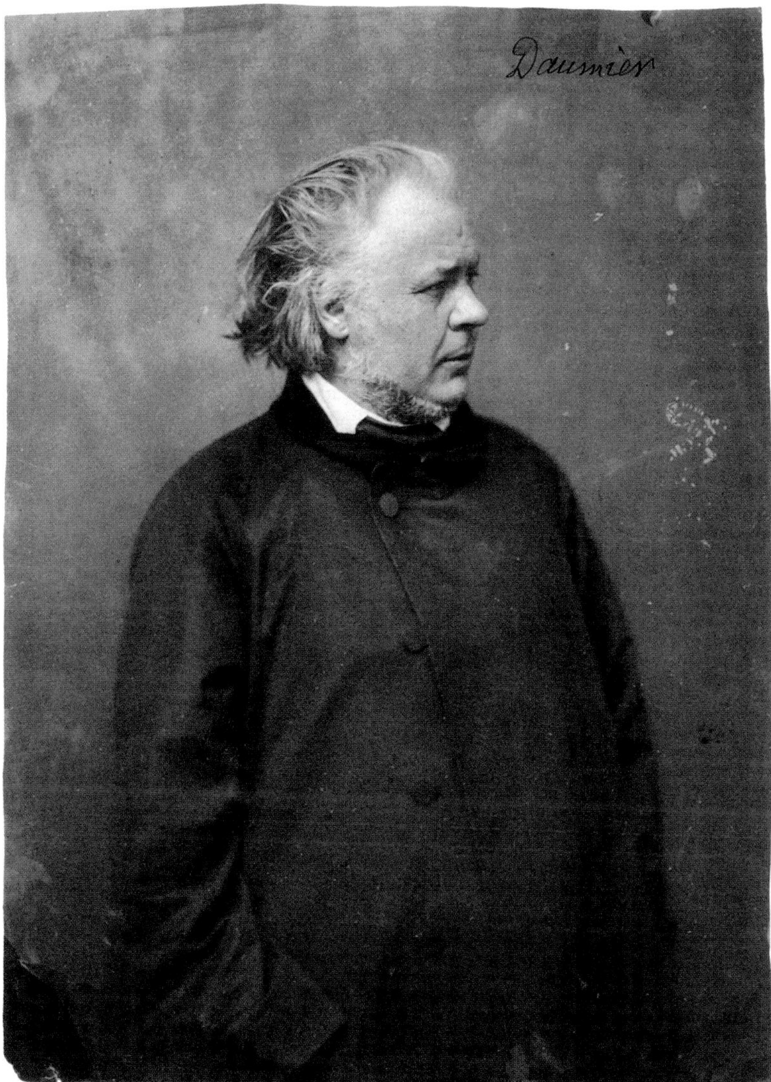
Daumier

Gustave Doré, Paris, 1856–8. Doré (1832–83) was amongst Nadar's intimate friends from the field of illustration and caricature. He posed for one of Nadar's earliest photographs and sat for him again in subsequent years. This portrait is one of a series done at the same sitting, where Nadar used Doré's scarf (and in another picture his cape) to match his chequered trousers. Not only does it enliven the composition, it also mitigates Doré's severe gaze with casual dandyish flair.

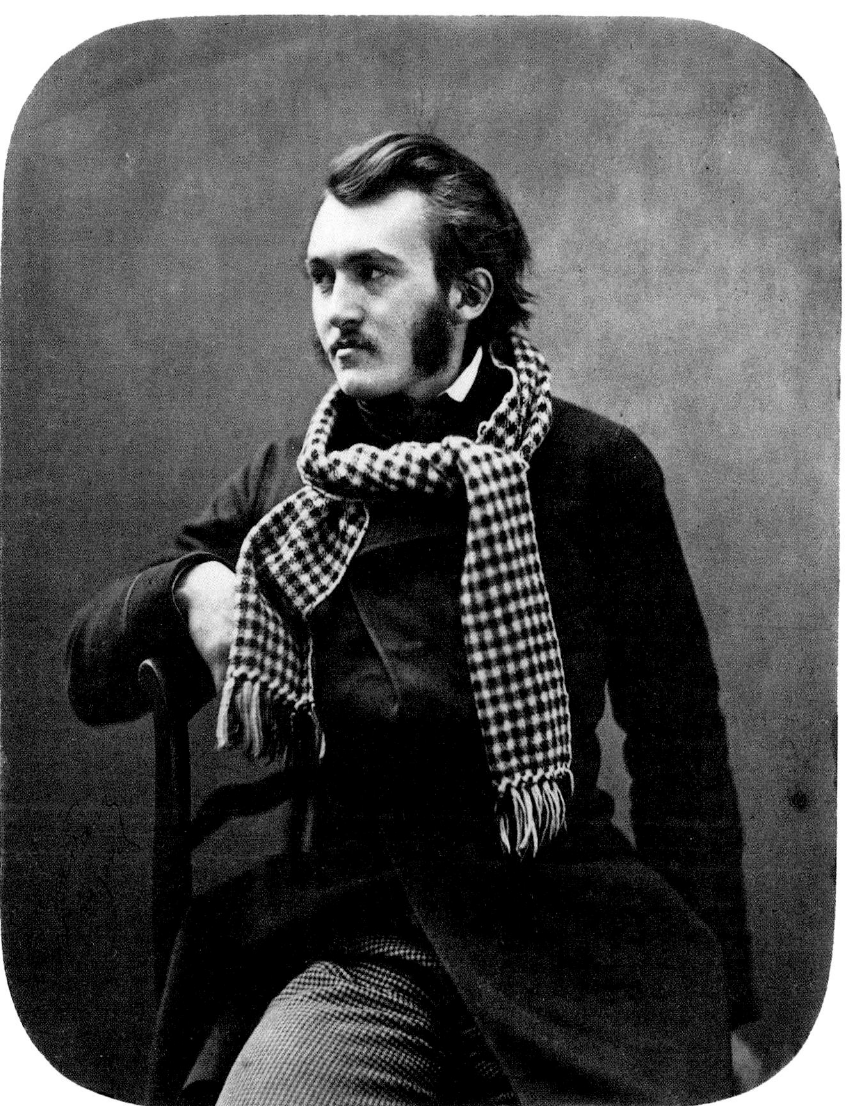

Gustave Doré, Paris, 1856–8. This later portrait of Doré, who has put on a little weight and is more conventionally groomed and dressed than in Nadar's earlier portraits of him, was made with electric light. Given the longer exposure time, he leans on one hand in order to keep from moving. This pose was in any case traditional in compositions meant to convey inner thoughtfulness, a characteristic often attributed to artists.

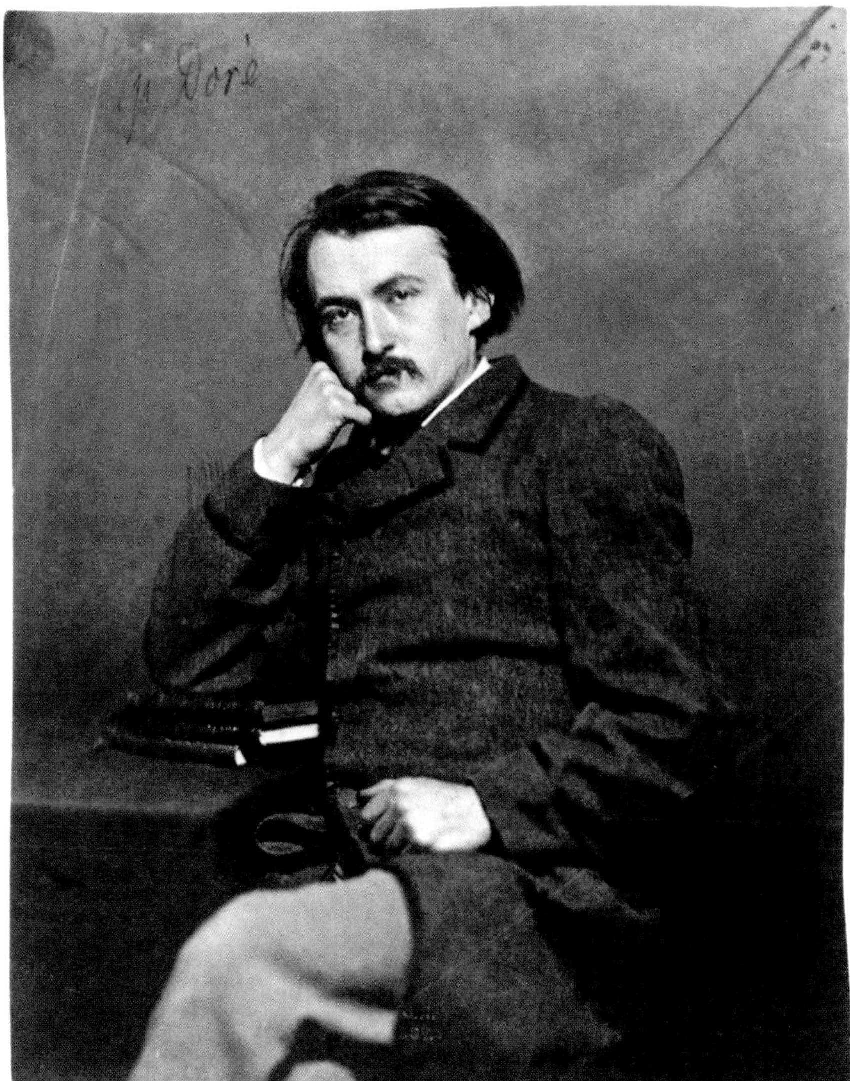
Doré

Jean Journet, Paris, 1856–9. Jean Journet (1799–1861) was a self-styled 'apostle' of Utopianism, who travelled across France on foot, preaching the communitarian ideals of socialist thinker Charles Fourier. Nadar has cast Journet as a religious visionary, gazing dramatically towards the heavens while wrapped only in what looks like a monk's habit. The unusually emphatic pose combines ironic reference to Journet's old-fashioned idealism with sympathetic admiration.

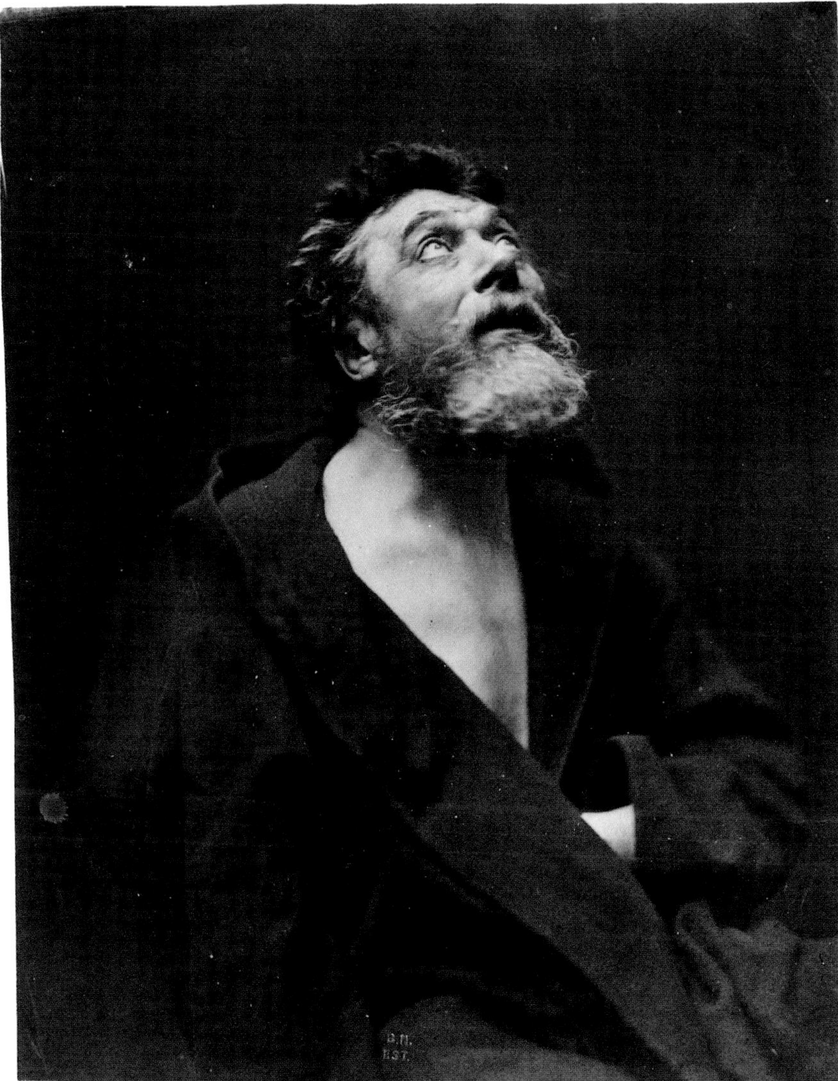
B.N.
EST.

Maria L'Antillaise, Paris, 1856–9. Known as 'Maria of the Antilles', this model posed several times in Nadar's studio. Depicting her with ample breasts exposed – enhanced by her flowery dress and kerchief – Nadar associates the exotic with traditional ideals of woman as nurturer and classical beauty. Yet he has not ignored her personality, which he portrays as sympathetic and thoughtful. Under his signature, the photographer has given the studio's address: 113 rue Saint-Lazare.

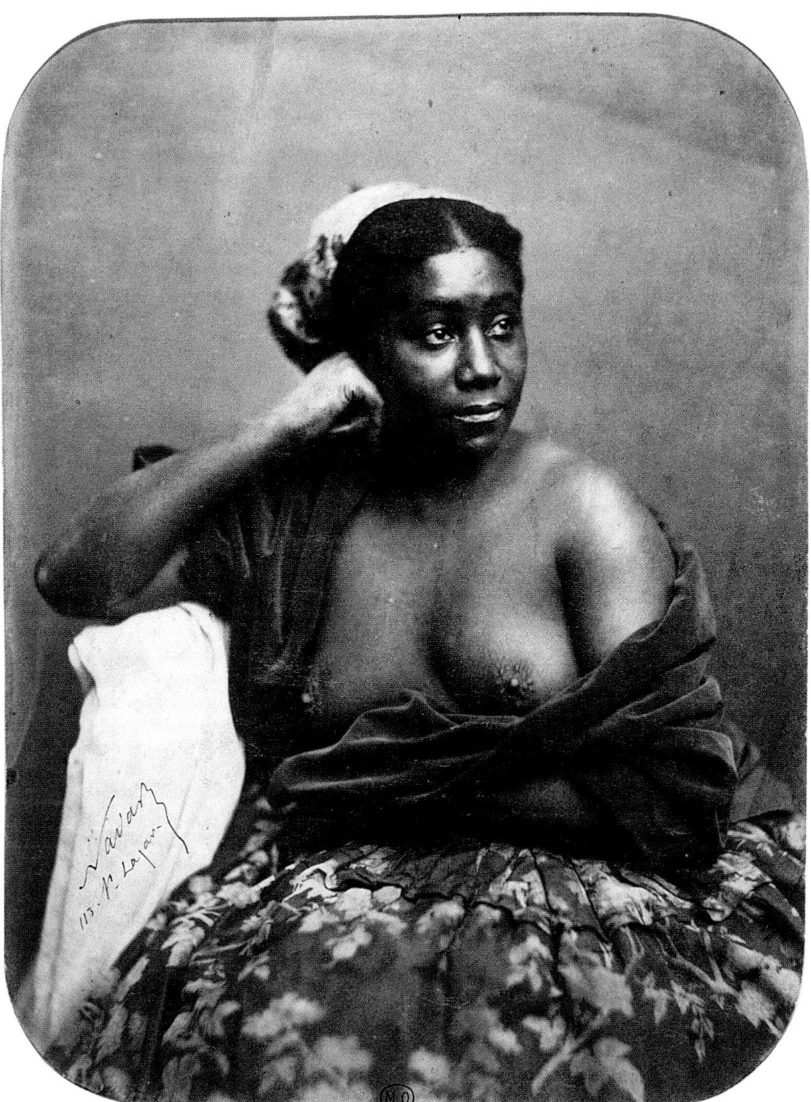
Nadar
113. R. St Lazare
M.O

Young Model, Paris, 1856–9. This portrait of a young model, about whom nothing is known, is remarkable for the interplay of her long wavy untied hair with the velvet folds of cloth enveloping her. The contrast is not only one of textures but of artistic traditions – a Pre-Raphaelite-like Realism combined with the sculptural classicism of the cloth-covered mass. The playful, experimental nature of the image is implicit in the model's tentative, bemused expression.

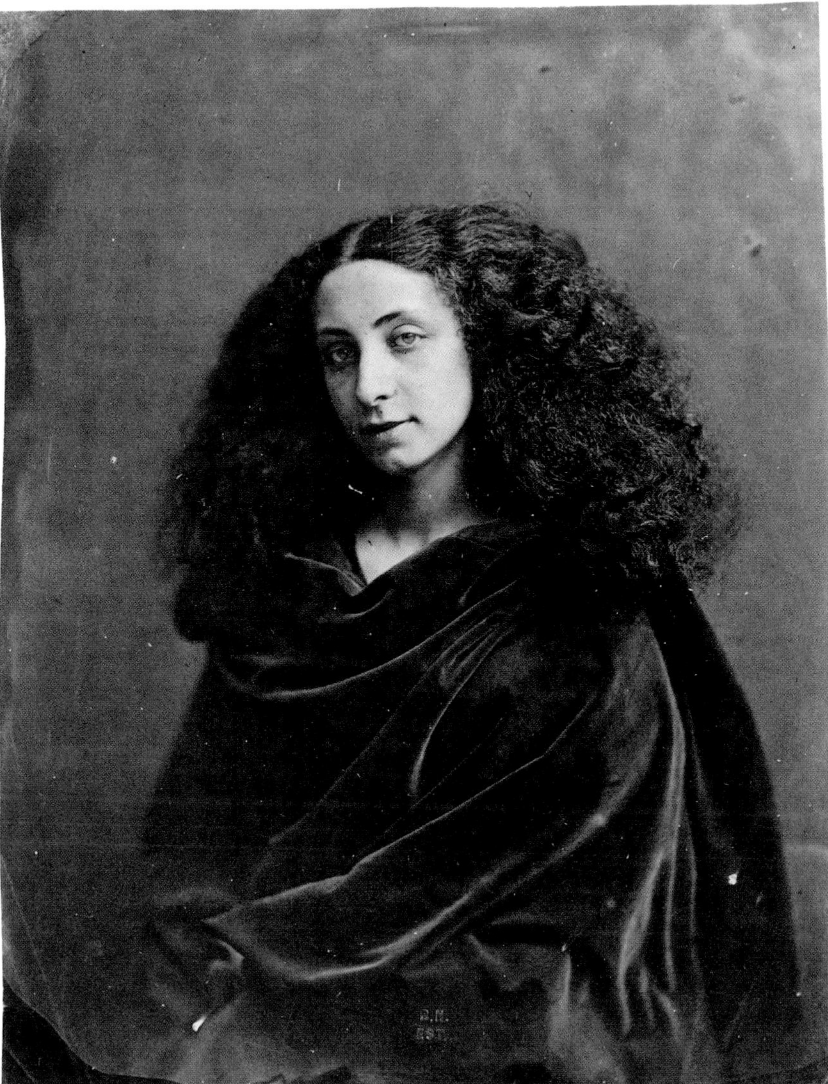

François Guizot, Paris, c.1857. Guizot (1787–1874) was a historian and political figure who served under both the Bourbon Restoration (1815–30) and the July Monarchy (1830–48). A Protestant who encouraged the middle classes to make themselves rich through work and responsibility, he had turned to the writing of history by the time of Nadar's portrait. Psychologically distant and formal in this pose, Guizot comes across as a man of high principle and patriotism, even though Nadar cannot have agreed with his politics.

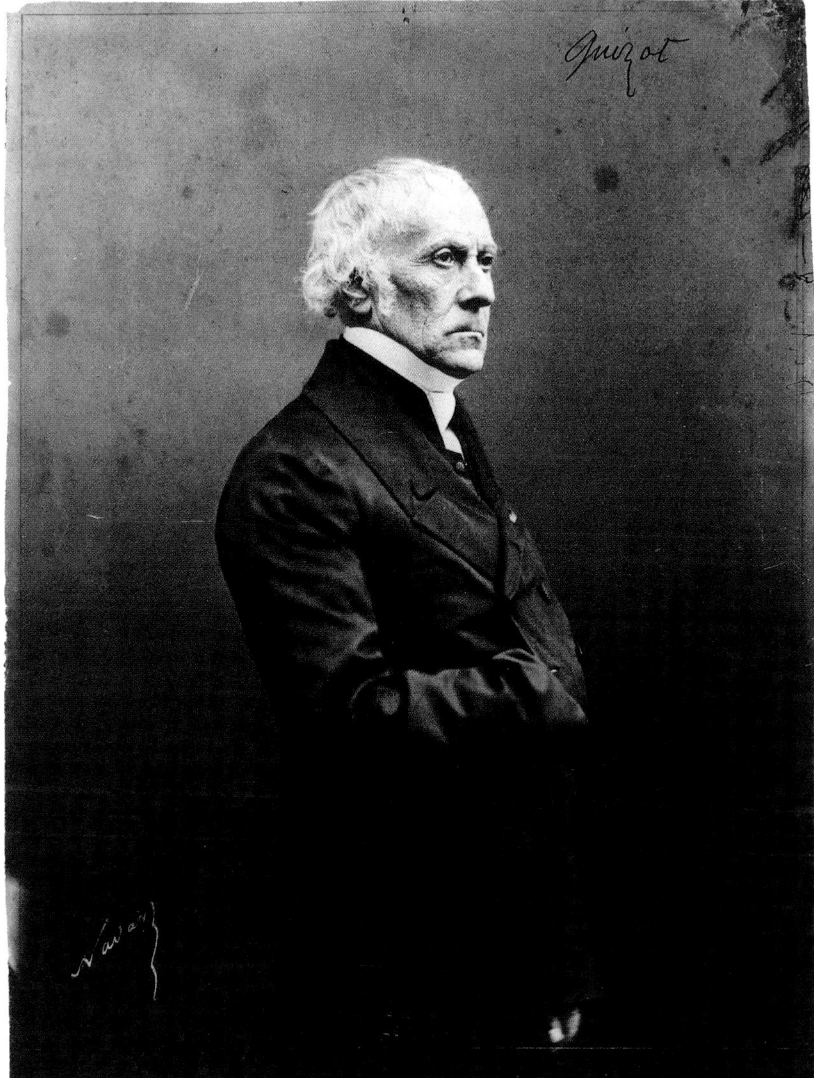
Guizot

Moses Saphire, Paris, c.1857. Moses Saphire (1795–1857), known as Maurice Gottlieb, was a Jewish–Hungarian satirist and cartoonist whom Nadar must have known through journalistic circles. Nadar's portrait records Saphire's distinctive features and mock serious expression in a way that in itself constitutes a caricature-like reference to the subject's literary and artistic personality.

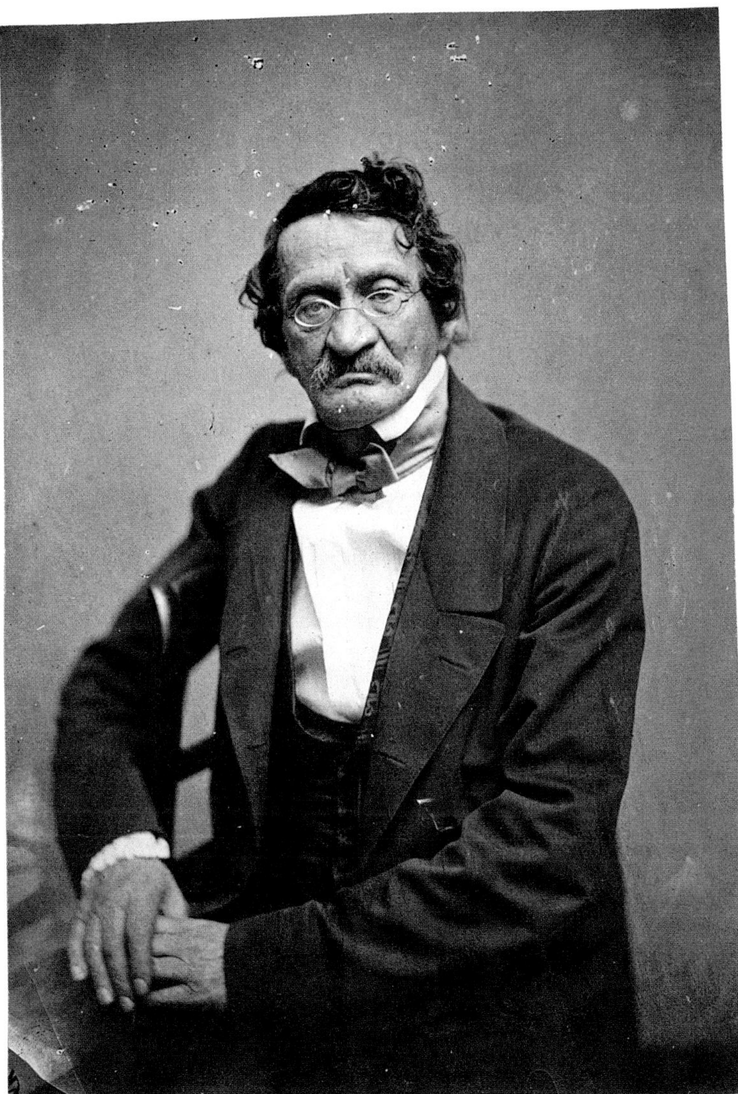

Eugène Delacroix, Paris, 1858. Delacroix (1798–1863) was the foremost Romantic painter of his time, widely known both for battling the artistic establishment and for his friendships with the most advanced writers and musicians of the period. By the time of this photograph, Delacroix had received important public commissions for government buildings and the Louvre. His gruff, self-assured expression tells of a man whose considerable accomplishments were earned through unflinching determination and effort.

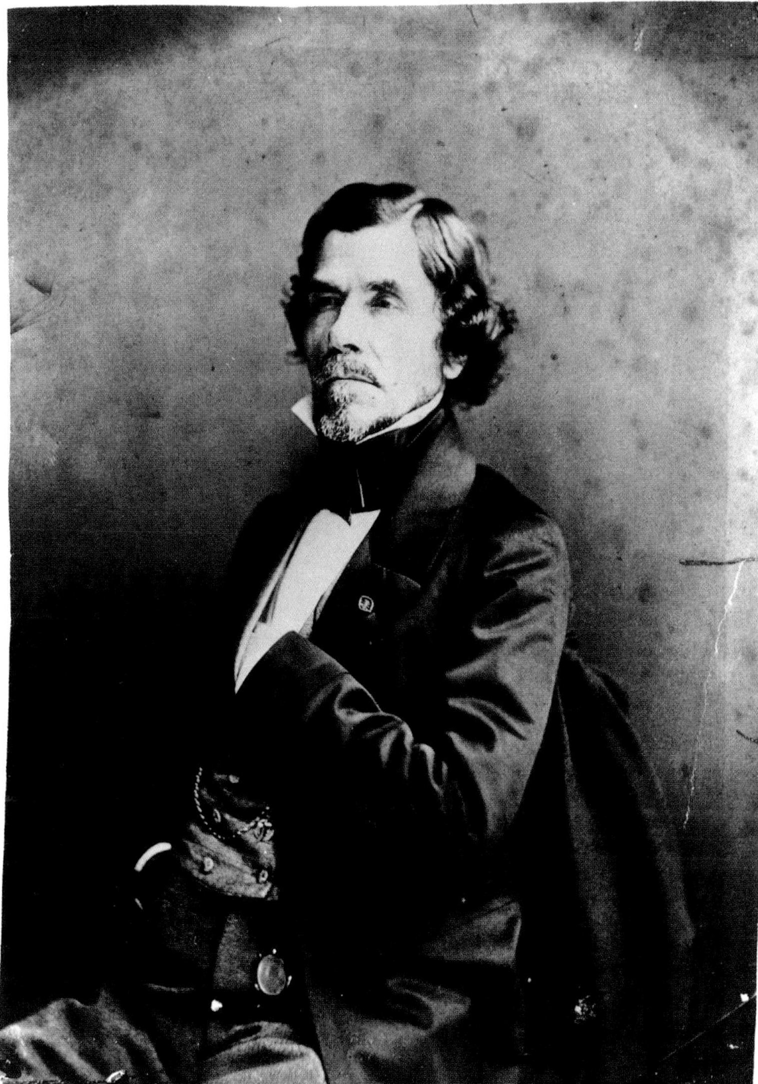

Adolphe Crémieux, Paris, c.1858. Crémieux (1796–1880) was a distinguished left-wing politician. Nadar must have admired his fight for the rights of the underprivileged, including the Jewish community, of which he was a leader. Crémieux was arrested after the *coup d'état* of Napoleon III; he subsequently became a leading opposition intellectual. Nadar's portrait may reveal a certain fatigue in his sitter, along with a knowing confidence in the justice of his principles.

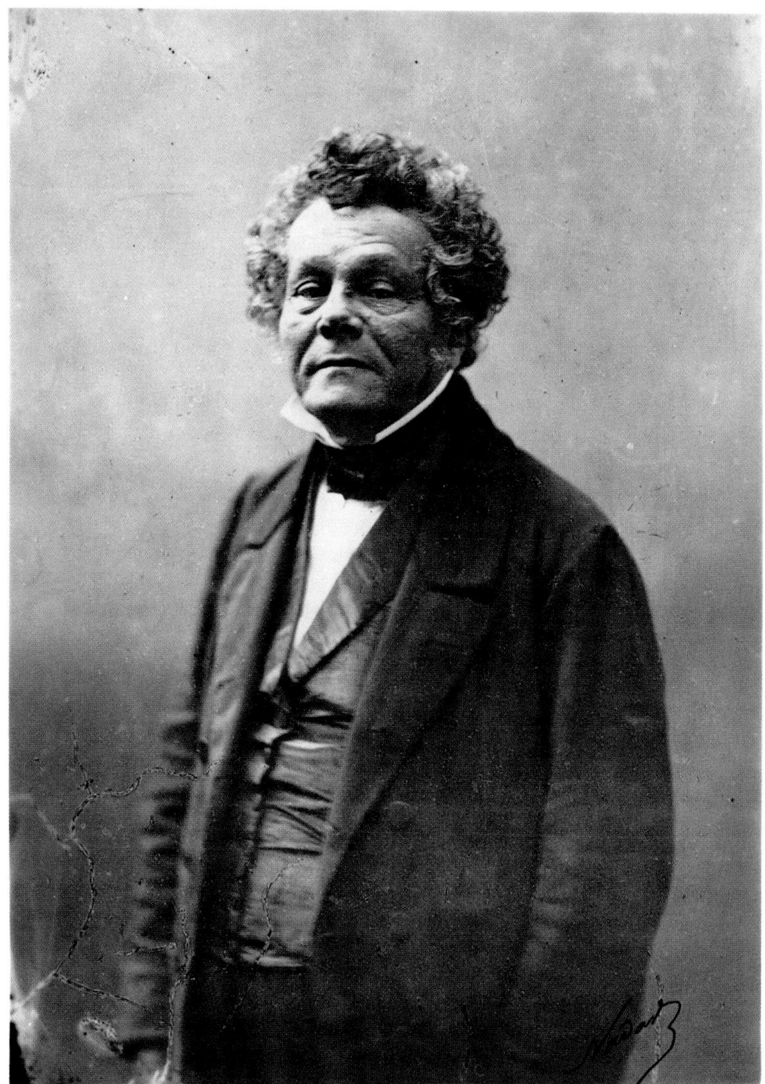

Juliette Adam, Paris, c.1858. Juliette Adam (1836–1936) had her first literary success with the novel *Blanche de Coucy* in 1858, followed by a life of Giuseppe Garibaldi, the Italian nationalist. She was subsequently known for her support of liberal and feminist causes. Nadar's portrait perfectly adheres to the standard representations of a bourgeois lady, with fan held in her lap, fashionable striped dress and embroidered shawl. Turned slightly towards the light coming from the left, she is also represented with a fine intelligence, appearing observant and ready to engage in discussion.

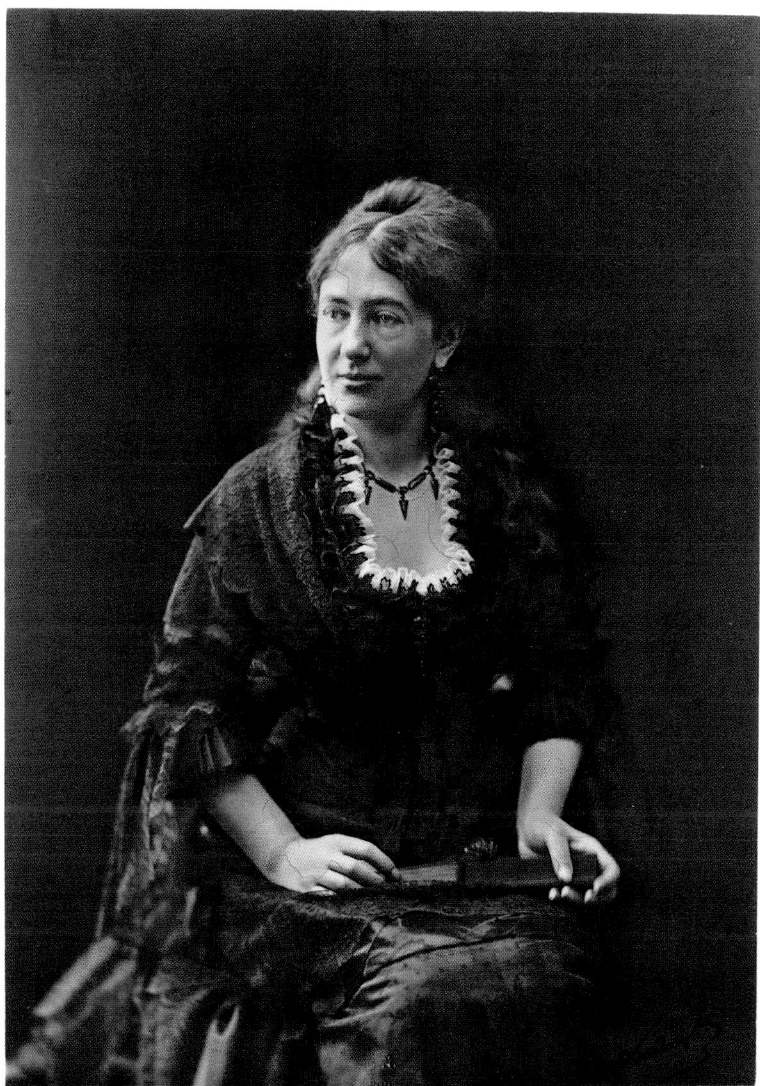

Isidore Severin, Baron Taylor, Paris, c.1858. Isidore Severin, Baron Taylor (1789–1879), the son of a naturalized Englishman, embarked on a military career but maintained a deep interest in the arts. Well-travelled and knowledgeable, he helped obtain the Luxor Obelisk from Egypt, which was erected at the Place de la Concorde in 1833. King Louis-Philippe commissioned him to collect works for his Spanish Museum, which was dispersed in 1848. Taylor was an important supporter of Nadar and was honorary President of the Heavier-than-Air Society, which met in Nadar's studio in the 1860s.

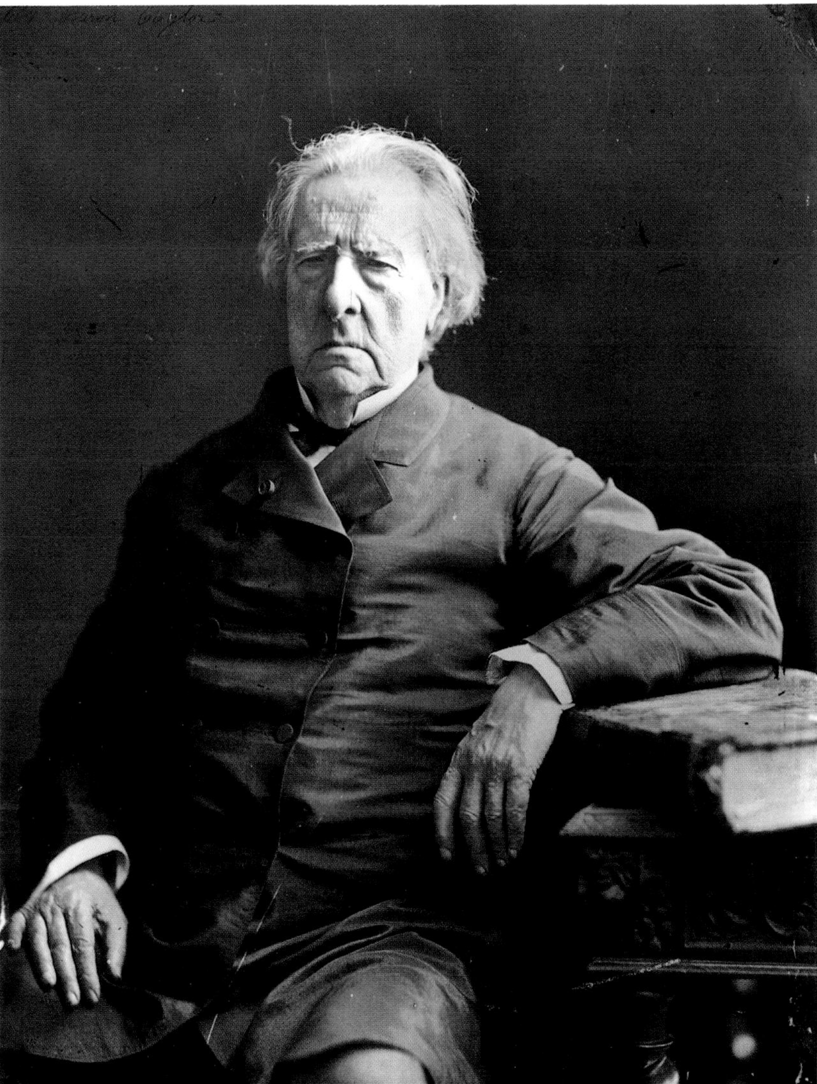

Emma Livry, Paris, c.1859. Emma Livry (1842–63) was the illegitimate daughter of a member of the Jockey Club and a sixteen-year old dancer. At her own debut at the age of sixteen, she caused a sensation. Only a full-length portrait would allow inclusion of the feet and shoes so central to the dancer's success. She wears the costume, including vine leaves in her hair, from a ballet performance of Félicien David's now forgotten *Herculaneum* of 1859.

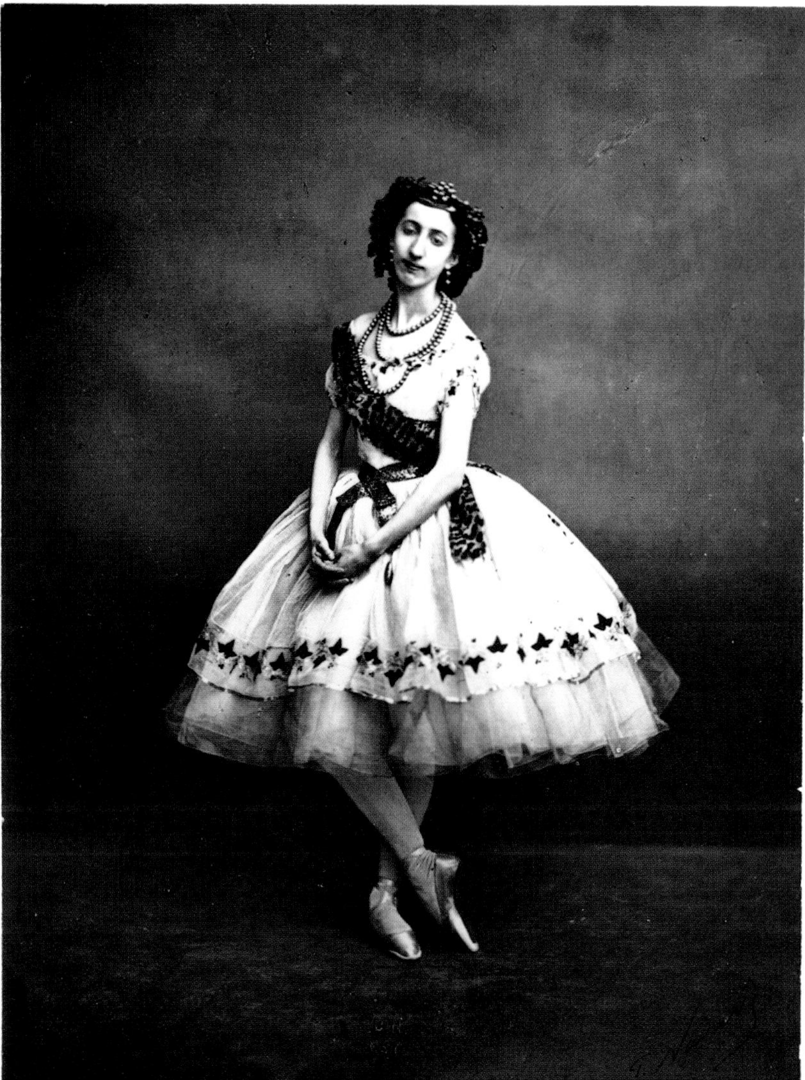

Self-portrait, Paris, c.1859. Nadar's many self-portraits are among his most interesting photographs. Not only was he able to control every element both of the take and pose, but he was free to experiment, as in this self-assured image done with artificial light. With his flamboyant attire and casual pose, Nadar comes across as very much the artist-dandy, while his wide-eyed look suggests both the power of his vision and the intensity of the lights into which he stares.

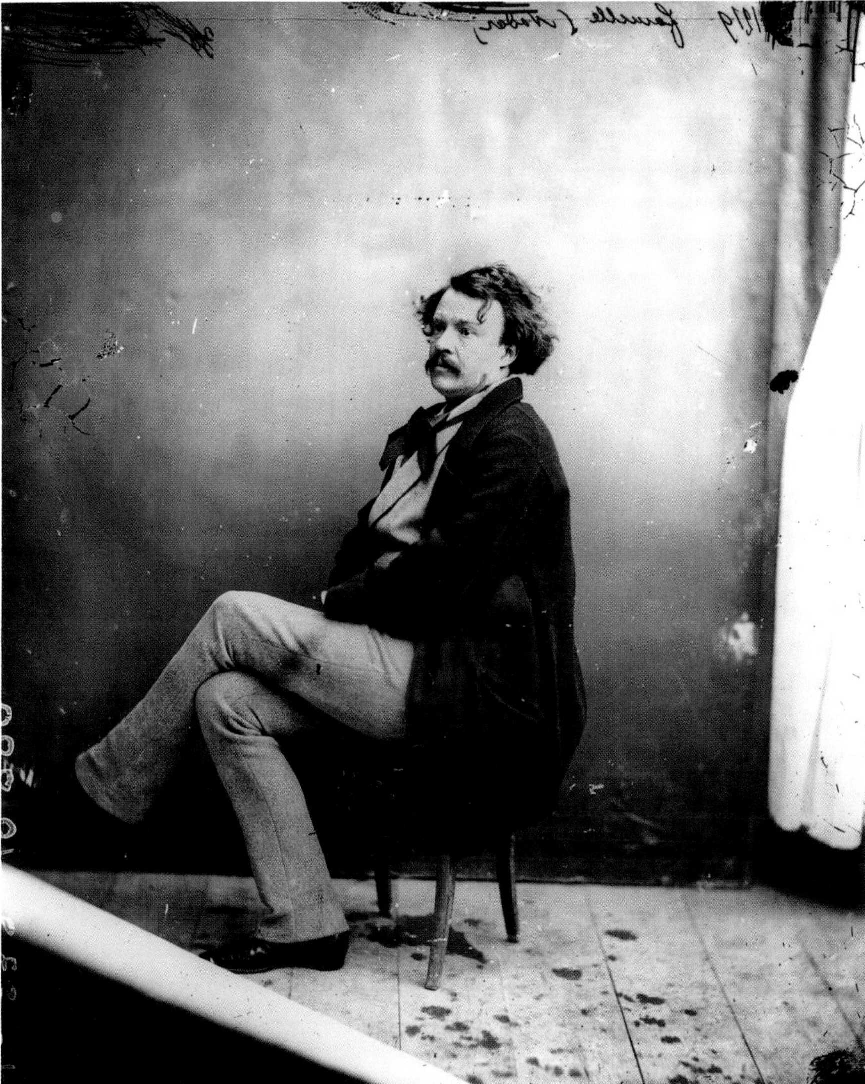

Giacomo Meyerbeer, Paris, 1860. Meyerbeer (1791–1864) (born Jakob Beer in Germany) was the composer of several operas, including the celebrated *Robert le diable* (1831), made in collaboration with Eugène Scribe as librettist, and *Les Huguenots* (1836). Appointed Director of Music in Berlin in 1842, Meyerbeer returned to Paris later in his career to compose anew, though with less success. The pose affected here suggests both rigorous administrator and thoughtful composer.

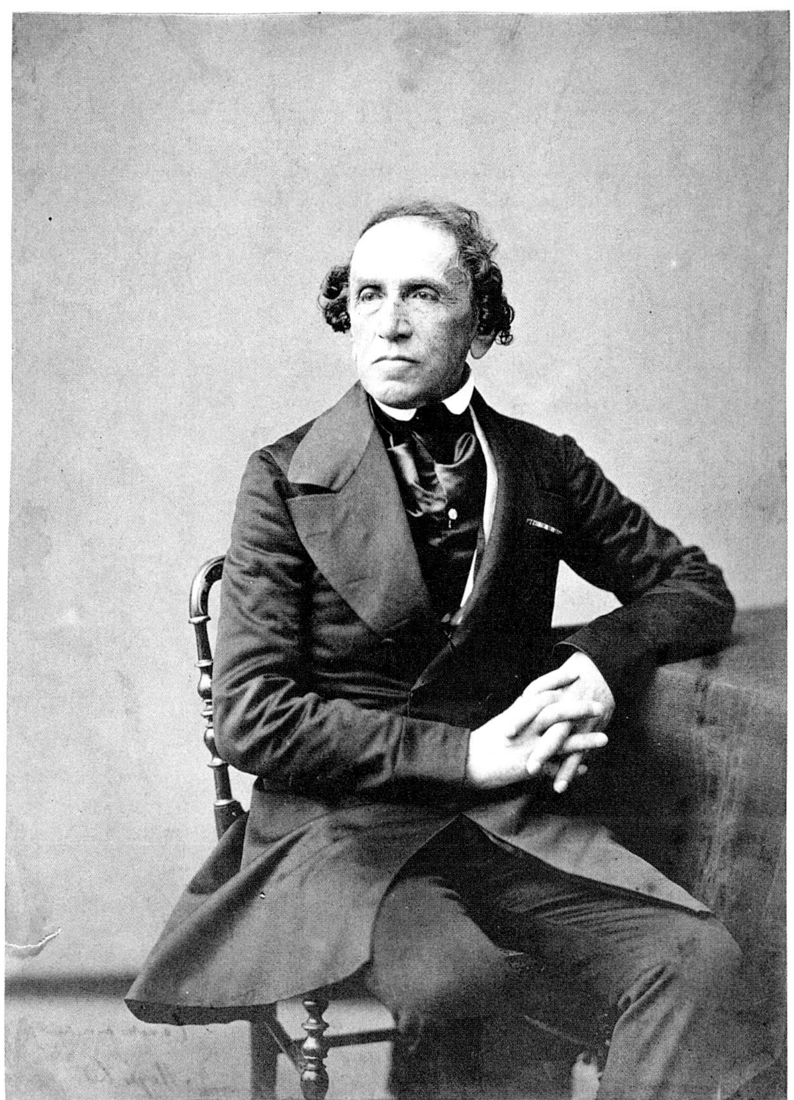

Hermaphrodite, Paris, 1860. Appealing to Nadar's interest in medicine and science, in 1860 Dr Armand Trousseau and surgeon Jules-Germain Maisonneuve commissioned a series of nine photographs of this unusual patient, a hermaphrodite. Along with some studies of human expressions that Adrien Tournachon had made for Dr Duchenne de Boulogne in 1854, these were among the first examples of the medical use of photography. No less sensational in our time than in Nadar's, these simple images use mass and shadow to imply the gravity of the phenomenon they record, preserving a semblance of dignity.

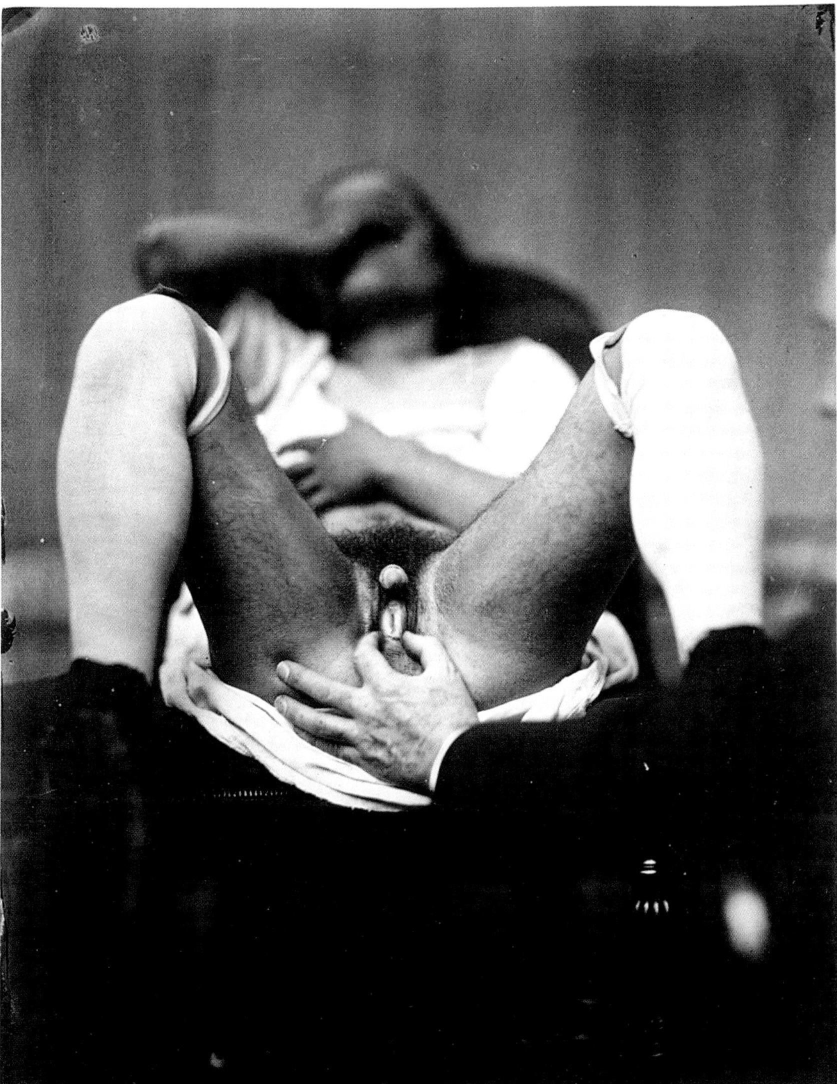

The Catacombs, Paris, 1861–2. In a series of seventy-three views, Nadar photographed the catacombs of Paris. He exhibited this one at the London International Exhibition, partly as a demonstration of his use of electric lights. Beyond the technical exploit, however, the piles of anonymous skulls and bones cannot help but evoke serious philosophical considerations. Although the catacombs were visited often by Parisians, the documentary clarity, stillness and close focus of Nadar's image creates a novel aesthetic experience of the *vanitas* theme, a meditation on mortality, with which skulls were traditionally associated in art.

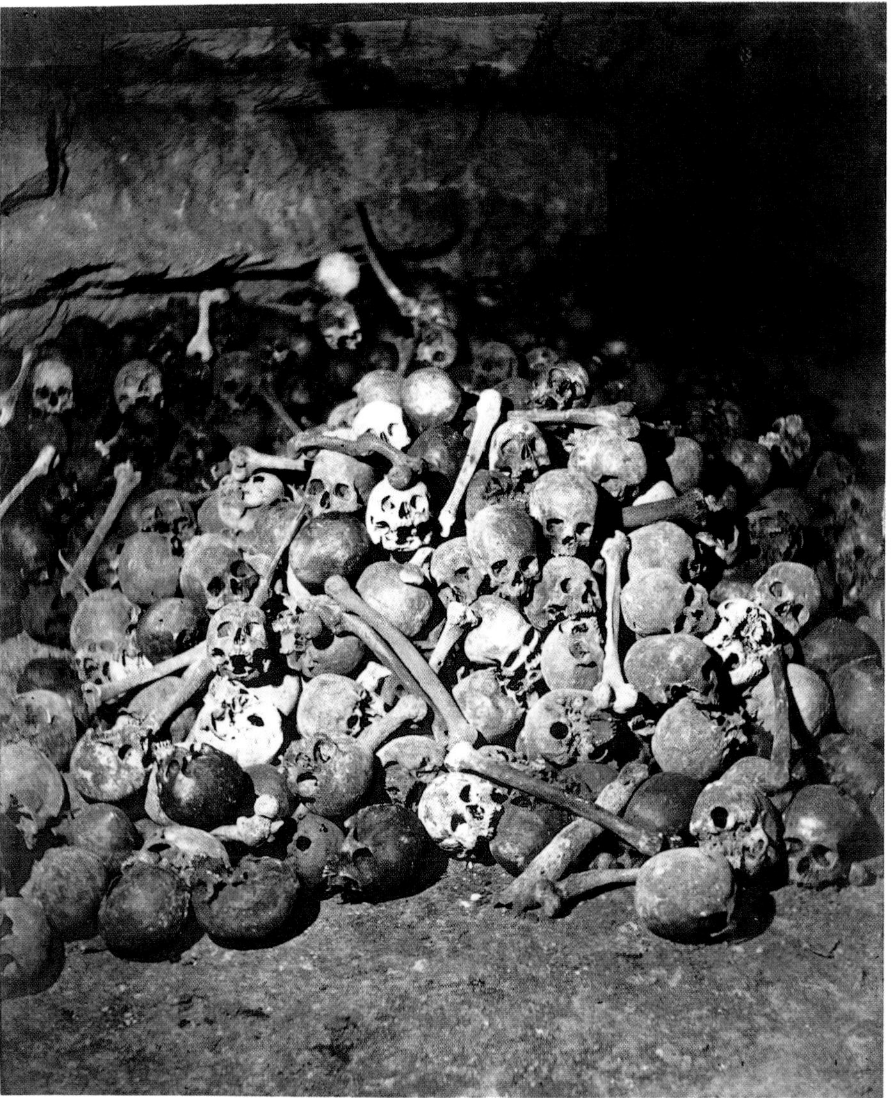

The Sewers, Paris, 1861–2. In his series of photographs of the sewers of Paris, Nadar used his battery-powered lights to record a world unknown to the ordinary Frenchman. Under Emperor Napoleon III's Prefect of Paris, Baron Haussmann, the city underwent extensive demolition and renovation, including the construction of the world's most modern sewer system. Many photographers were employed above ground in recording the development of transportation and urban infrastructure. It was Nadar's idea to take his camera to these underground passageways, with their pipes and rails suggesting the machine-like inner anatomy of the modern metropolis.

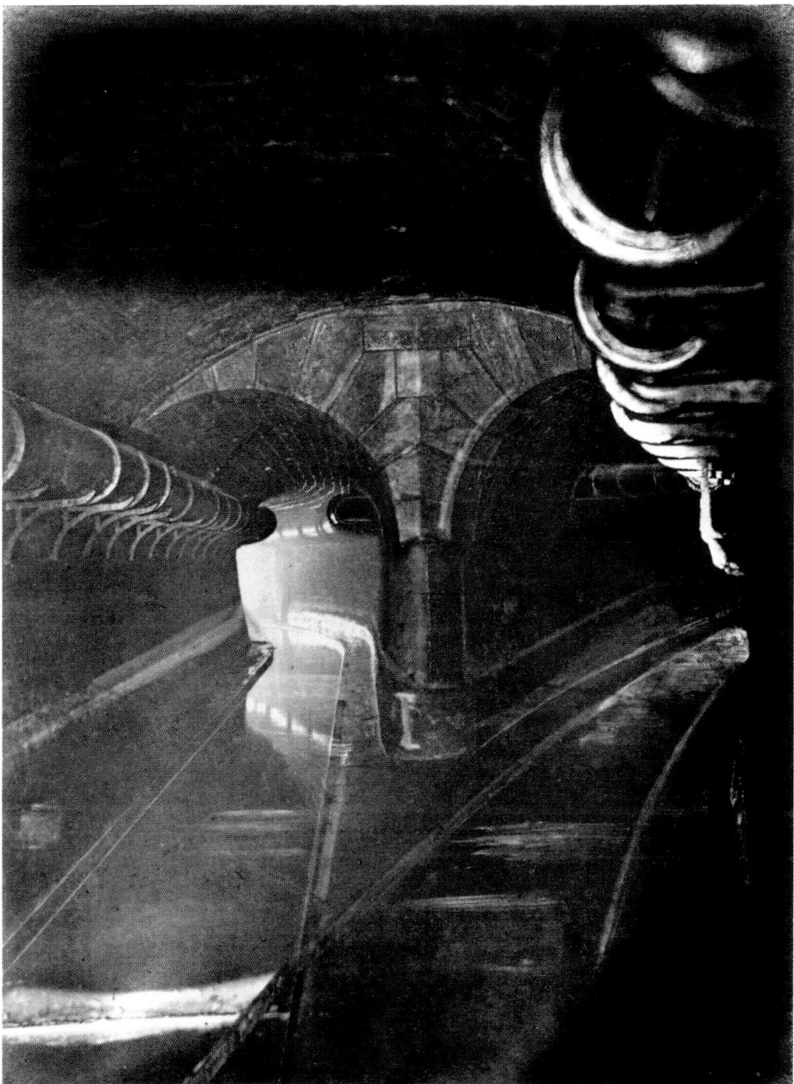

Helicopter, Paris, 1863. As evidenced by this photograph of an experimental helicopter, invented by the viscount Ponton d'Amécourt, Nadar's scientific interests led him to explore the principles of heavier-than-air flight. Whether this or other similar apparatuses that he photographed ever flew successfully is unknown. In the simple isolation of Nadar's photograph, this one proffers a delightful still life, evocative of the aspirations it embodies as well as elegance of design.

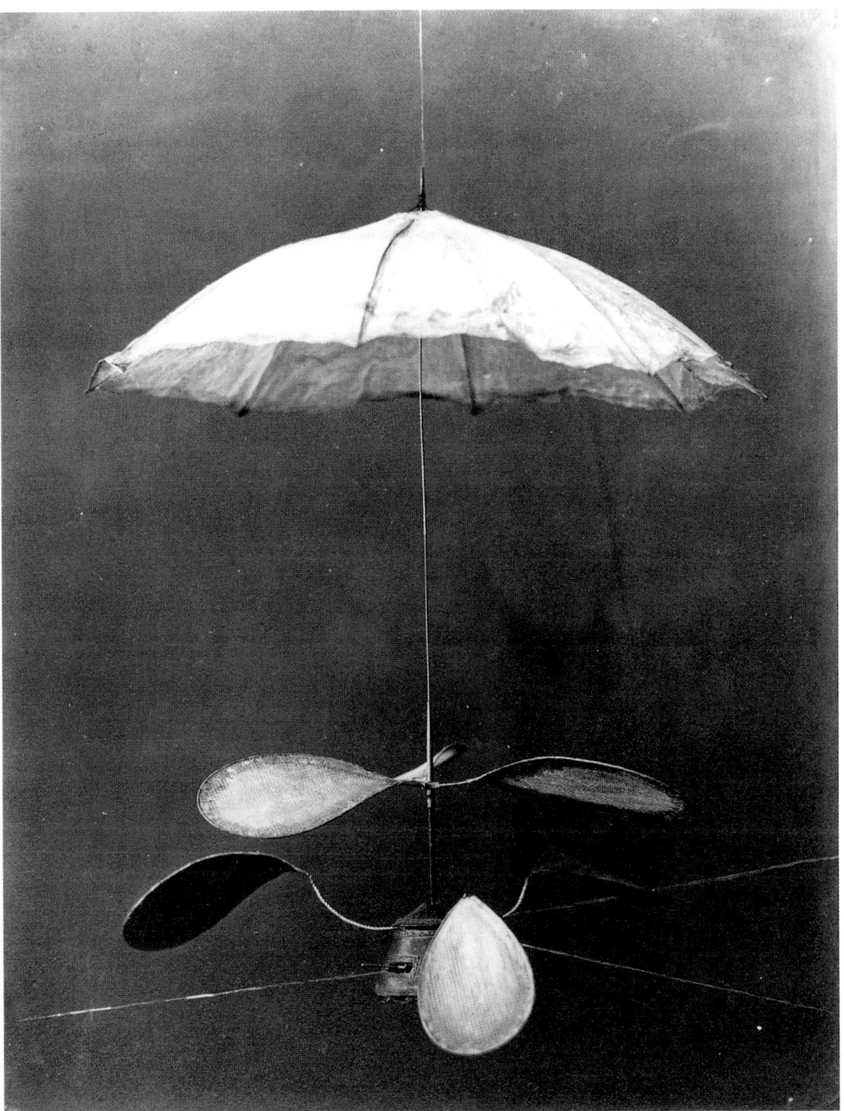

Pierre-Joseph Proudhon, Paris, 1862. Proudhon (1809–65) was France's most radical political thinker in the 1850s and 1860s, a staunch opponent of the Second Empire and an advocate of the redistribution of wealth. His book of 1842, *What is Property?*, gave the simple answer 'Property is theft!' This portrait was executed in Nadar's new studio on the boulevard des Capucines, as evidenced by the more ornate chair he uses as a prop. Proudhon leans on a thick tome, undoubtedly one of his many voluminous publications.

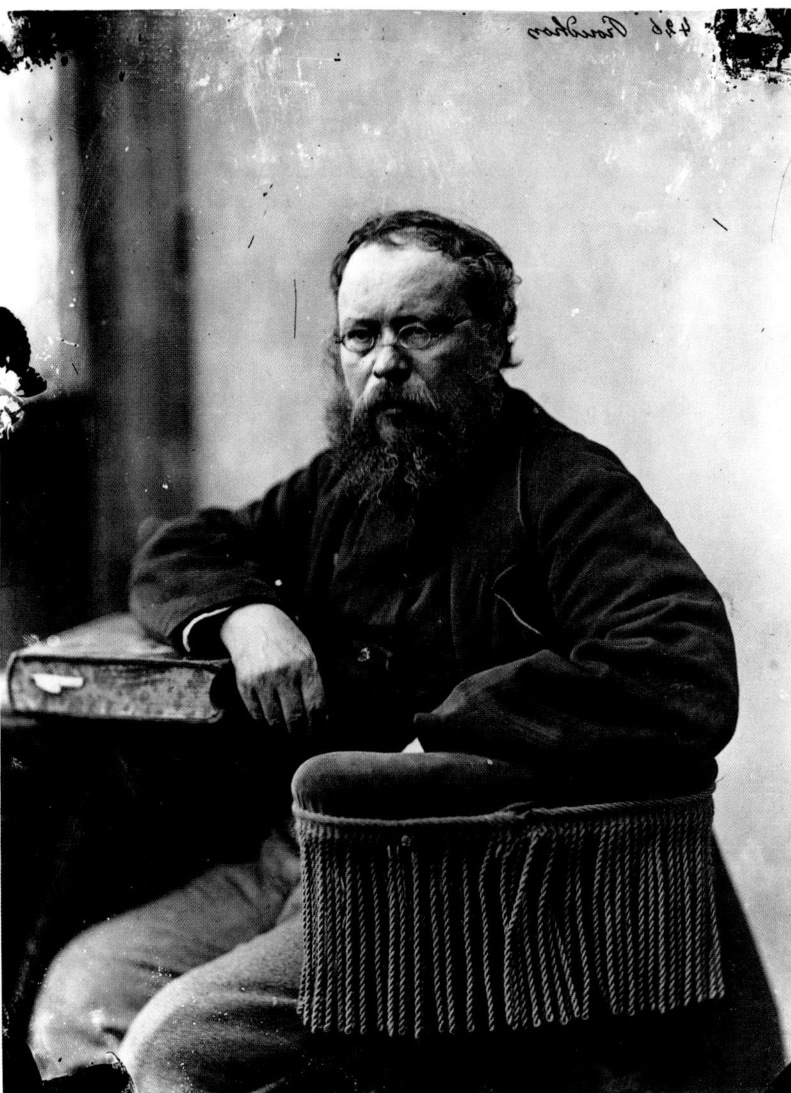

Mikhail Bakunin, Paris, c.1863. The Russian anarchist Mikhail Bakunin (1814–76), best known for extolling the creativity of destructive forces, was banished from Russia in 1844, then arrested and sent to Siberia, from which he eventually escaped. In his travels around Europe, where he wrote while attempting to organize revolutionary actions, he visited Paris several times. Nadar's portrait suggests the odd combination of Bakunin's aristocratic origins (note his expensive clothing) and faith in the ordinary peasantry.

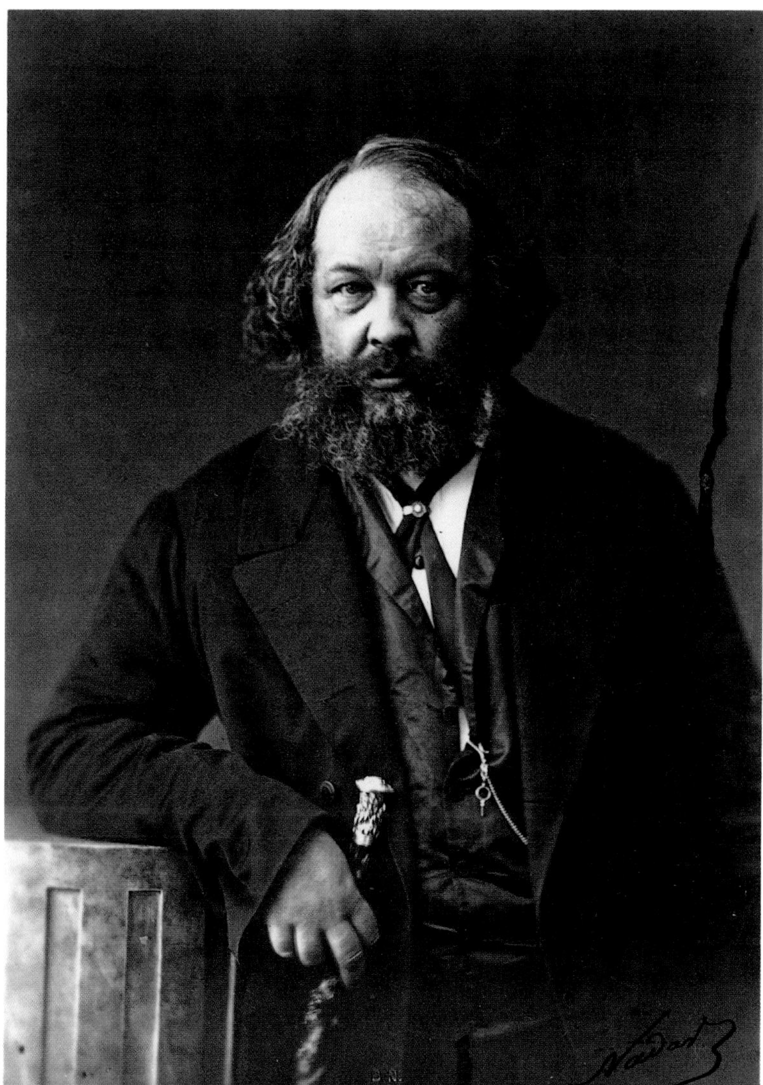

Edouard Manet, Paris, 1863–4. Manet (1832–83) became the most notorious painter of his day when he showed his *Déjeuner sur l'herbe* at the Salon des Refusés in 1863. Manet's background was high bourgeois, and he affected a somewhat dandyish appearance at the same time as challenging the artistic establishment. Nadar's photograph was probably taken sometime after the Salon exhibition and shows the painter astride Nadar's armchair in a gesture of seriousness and determination.

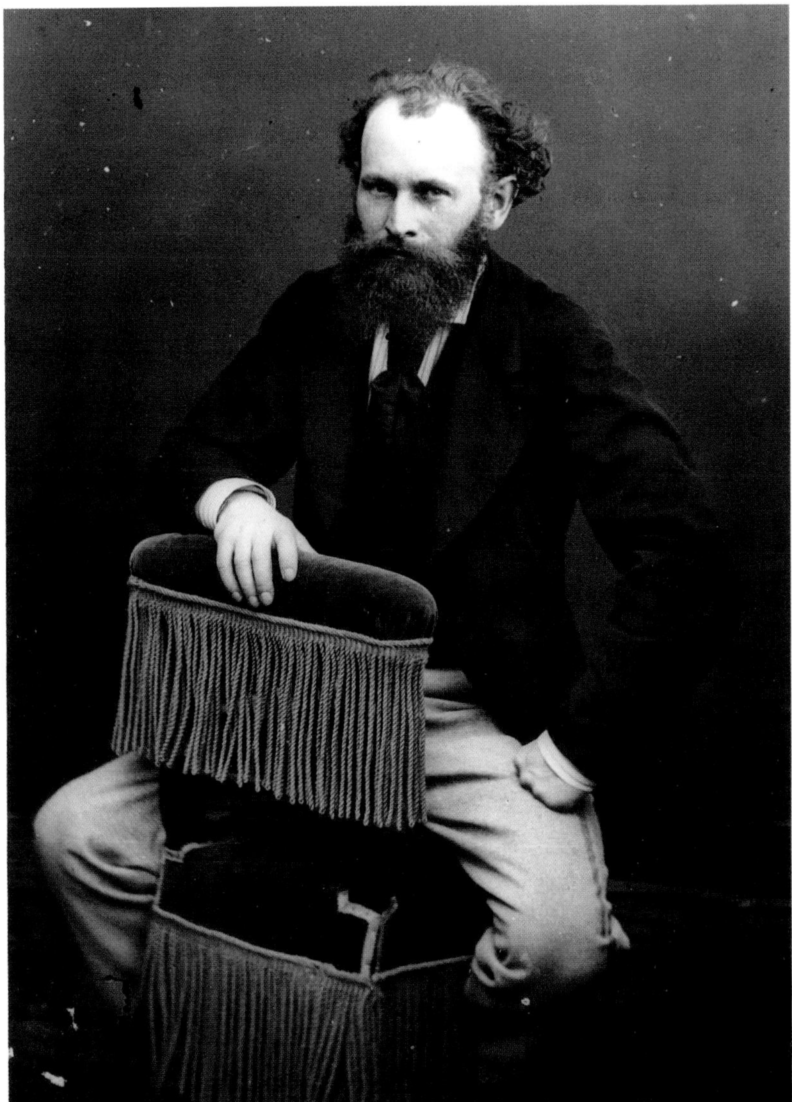

George Sand, Paris, 1864. George Sand (1804–76) was the pseudonym of Aurore Dupin, one of France's leading novelists and certainly its most famous woman of letters. She had become notorious for wearing trousers and smoking cigars, as well as for amorous liaisons with Frédéric Chopin and Franz Liszt. Nadar had long admired her; he placed her statue at the head of the cortège of luminaries in his *Panthéon* lithograph. Among the qualities in Sand that attracted him was her sentimental leftist politics, expressed in writings by extolling the virtues of country folk. Nadar knew Sand well – she was godmother to his son – and in another photograph she poses with a Louis XIV wig that Nadar himself had worn to a costume ball.

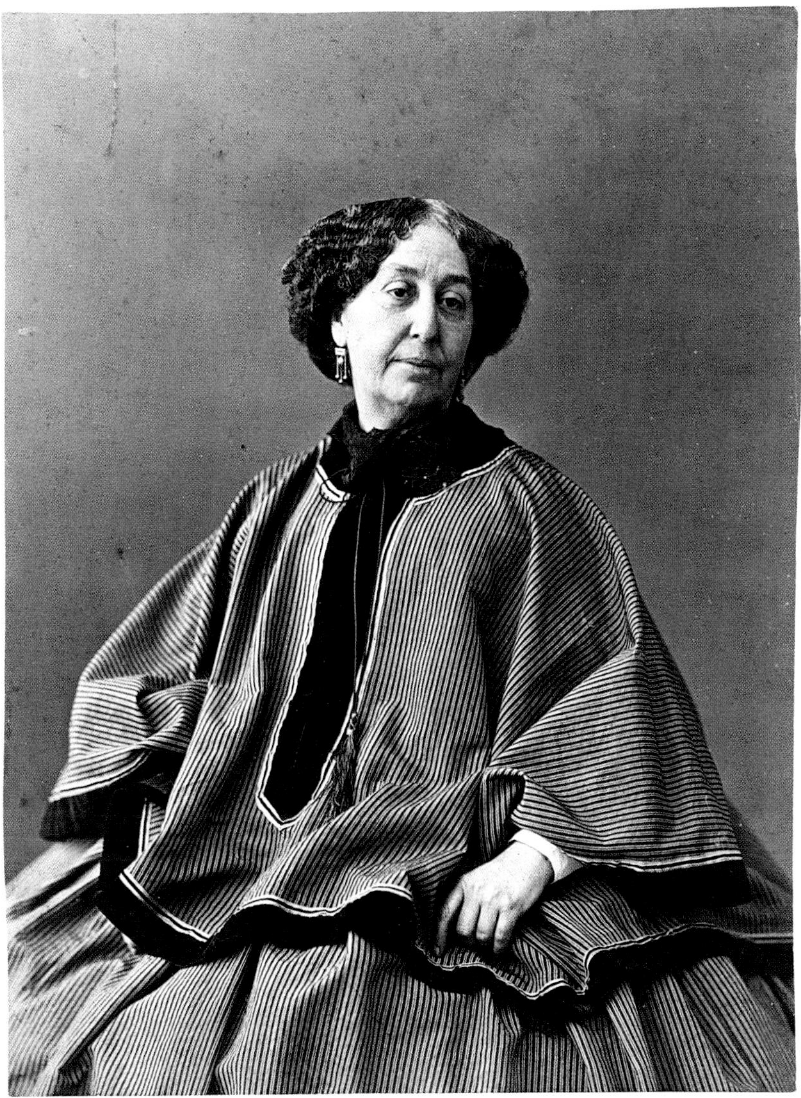

Sarah Bernhardt, Paris, c.1864. Bernhardt (1844–1923) was the ravishing illegitimate child of a Jewish oculist's daughter and a naval officer. Her studies at the Paris Conservatory and her appointment to the Comédie Française were facilitated by her aunt, a well-connected courtesan. In this photograph of about 1864, she is shown well before her sensational theatrical appearances of several years later. She is about twenty years old, yet her expression has some of the melancholy frailty that was to make her so seductive on the stage.

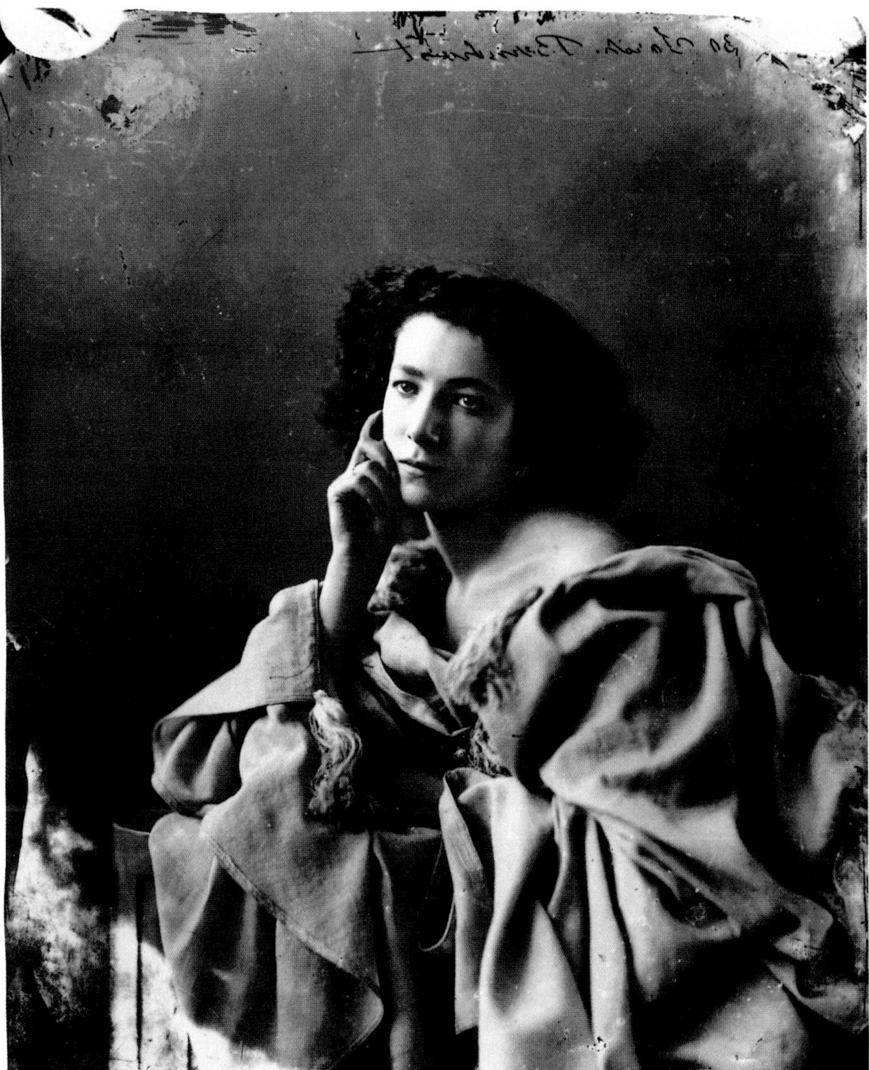

Sarah Bernhardt, Paris, 1864. Another photograph of Sarah Bernhardt, who became a regular client of the Nadar studio later on, has the simplicity of classical portraiture. Nadar has deliberately cultivated this idea by juxtaposing her with his cut-off column prop and by calling attention to the cameo earring she wears. The unadorned draperies covering her ostensibly nude body add mass to her delicate frame. In what is surely Nadar's most endearing image of the actress, she appears like a hesitant sibyl.

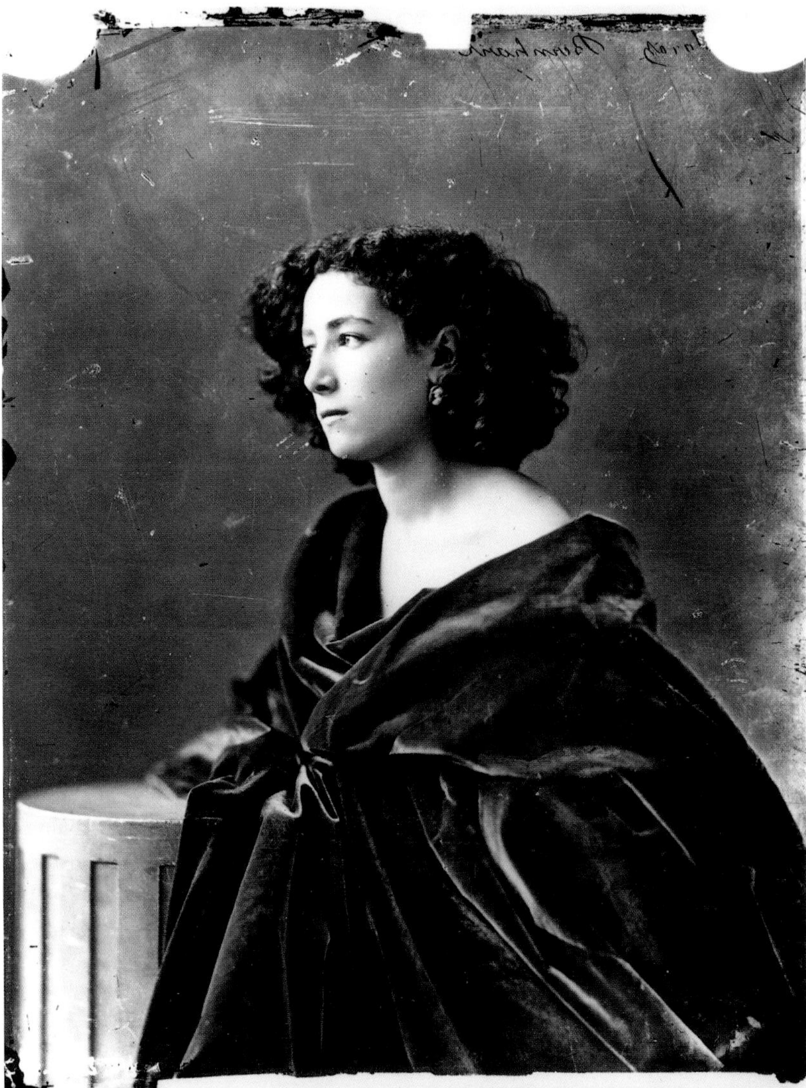

Carlotta Grisi, Paris, 1865. Carlotta Grisi (1819–99), the dancer for whom the ballet *Giselle* was written, was photographed by Nadar well after her retirement from the stage in 1853. She is not shown as a performer but as an elegant lady of the bourgeoisie. The smaller size of this portrait was for making cartes-de-visite. Producing four images at a time, they were cheaper and more portable than the full plate. To keep up with the competition, Nadar had begun using this format in the 1860s.

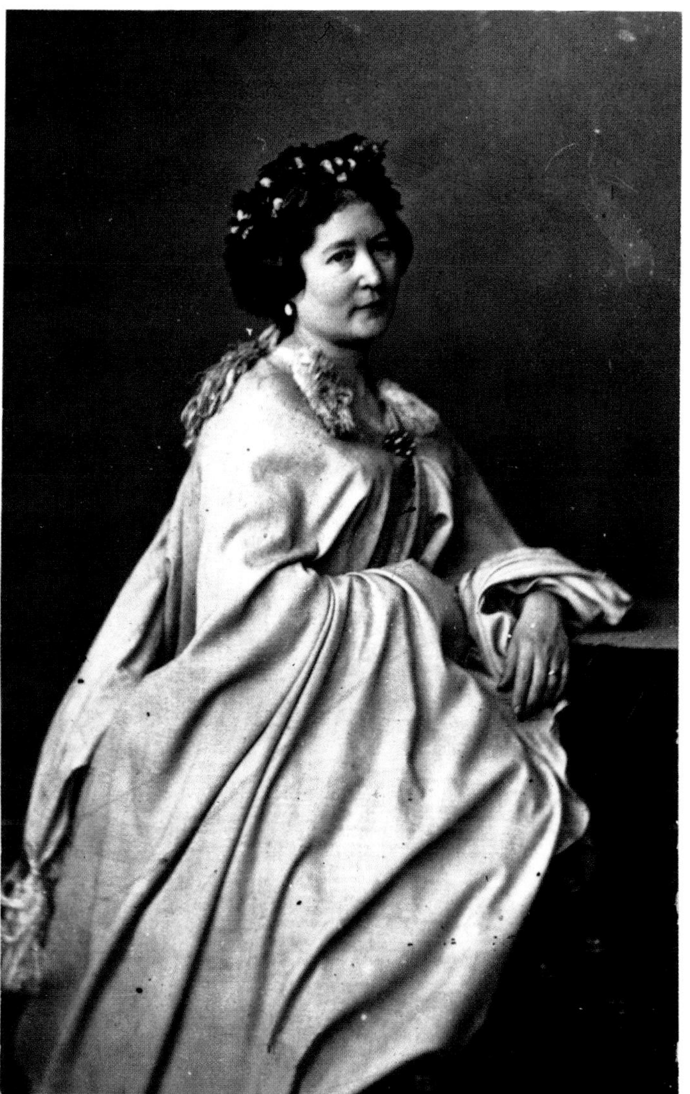

Jules Champfleury, Paris, c.1865. Champfleury (1821–89) was a leading member of the artistic bohemia of the 1840s, out of which Realism in art and literature grew. He wrote novels and short stories in provincial settings in the vein of George Sand, and his interest in the visual arts led him to collect popular imagery and rediscover the Le Nain brothers, seventeenth-century painters from his home town of Laon. He is known for his close friendships with the notorious painter Courbet and the scandalous Baudelaire, both of whom he fervently supported in the press.

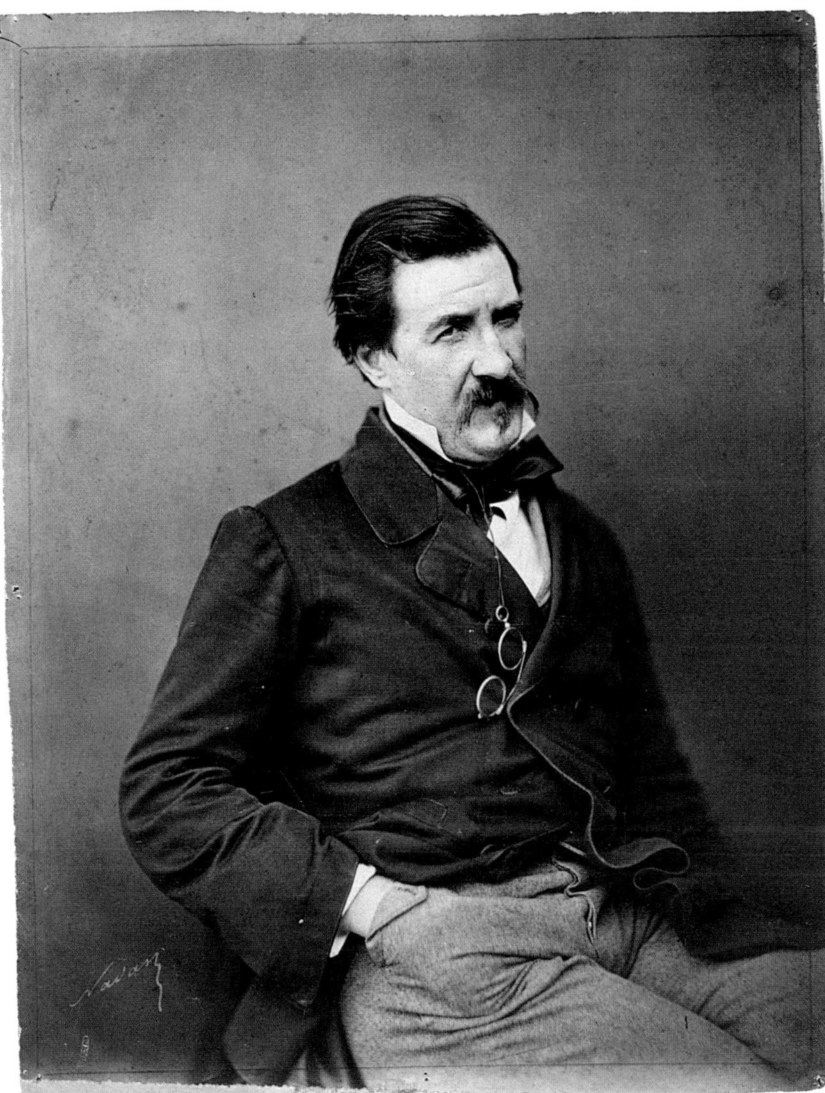
Nadar

Gustave Courbet, Paris, c.1866. Courbet (1819–77) was the leader of Realism in art, controversial both for his political views and for his artistic representations of the common man. Nadar shows him here in a somewhat conventional pose, which conveys relatively little of the painter's reputation as a coarse provincial firebrand. The truth is that by the mid-1860s, Courbet was trying to ingratiate himself with the establishment – that is, until the fall of the Second Empire led to his militant participation in the Commune's takeover of the city of Paris, and his subsequent exile to Switzerland.

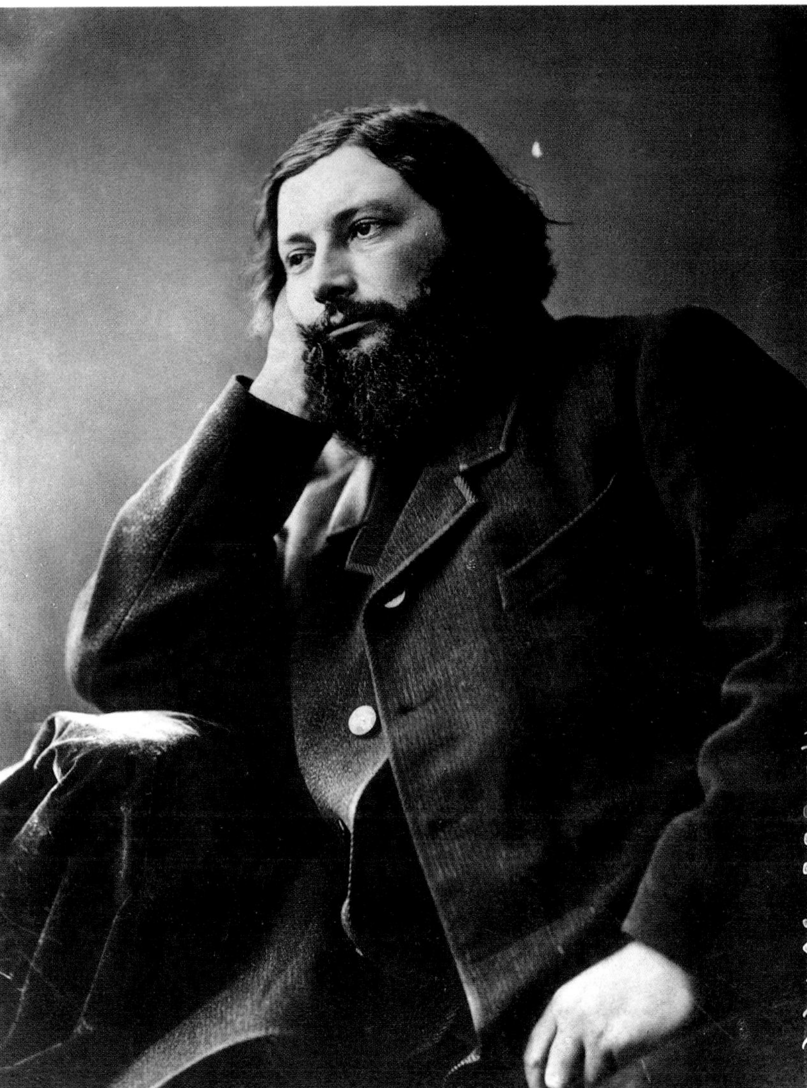

View of the Arc de Triomphe from a Balloon, Paris, 1868. Nadar's interest in balloon flight led to the first experiment in aerial photography. The multiple carte-de-visite format of this image suggests that he expected to exploit such photographs commercially. It is a view of the Arc de Triomphe, one of Paris's most celebrated monuments, erected at the crossroads of the most modern section of an expanding city. In thus combining the technological modernity of aerial photography with the subject matter of modern urbanization, the image is the other side of the coin to Nadar's photographs of the Paris sewers.

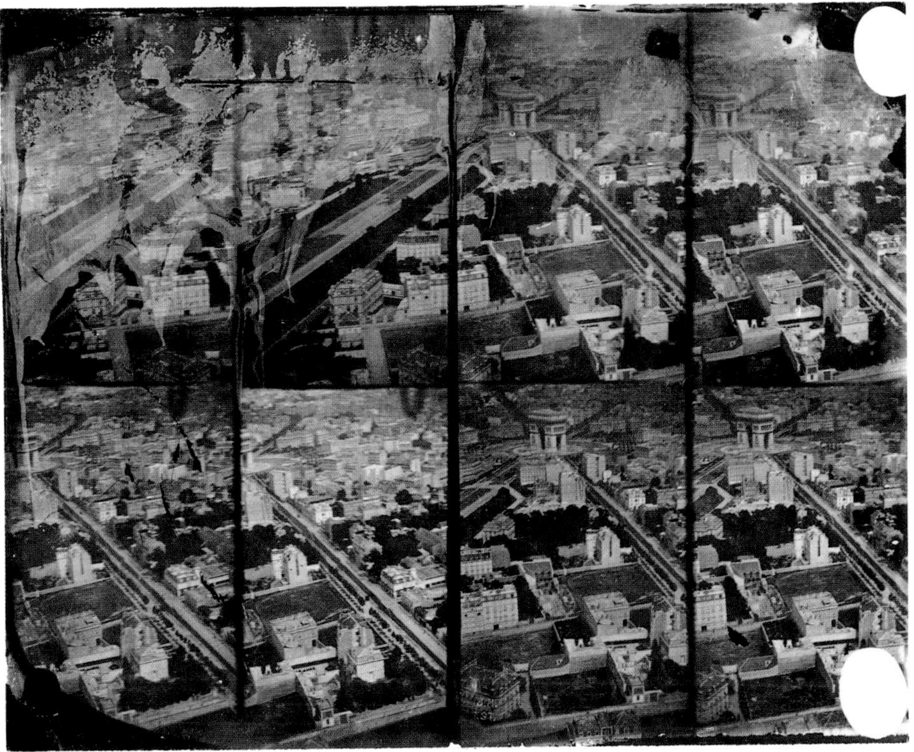

Jacques Offenbach, Paris, 1875. Born in Cologne to a synagogue cantor, Jacques Offenbach (1819–80) became a central figure in the Parisian world of entertainment. He is now best remembered for his posthumously performed opera *The Tales of Hoffmann* (1881) and was the composer of over 100 operettas. He went from being the Music Director of the Comédie Française to open his own theatre, the Bouffes-Parisiens, in 1855. A long-time friend of Nadar, he appears good-humoured and successful in his luxurious fur-collared coat, despite the decline of his career in his final decade.

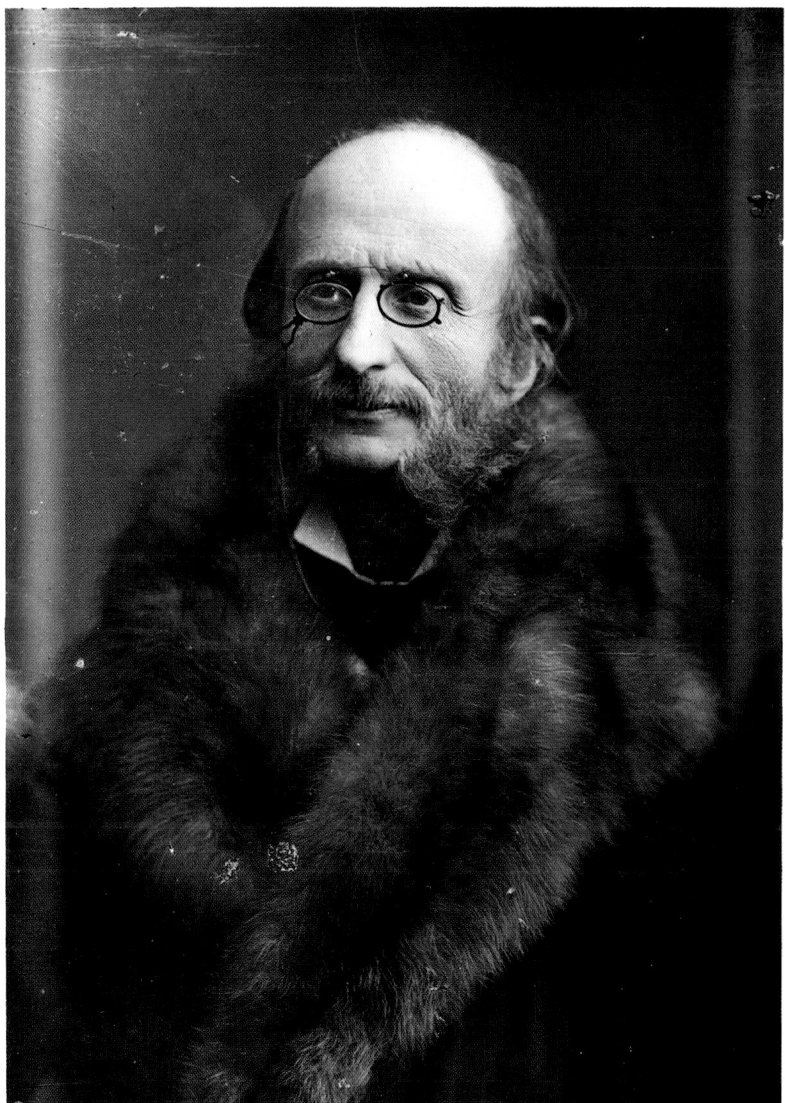

Charles Garnier, Paris, 1877. Charles Garnier (1825–98) was the architect of the monumental Paris Opéra, which he designed under the Second Empire. It is often thought to embody the excess of this period, although it did not open until 1875 and was only completed in 1884. The building became the centre of fashionable society and made its young architect a celebrity. In this portrait, Garnier adopts the thoughtful pose so often associated with artists, but his gaze is that of the more straightforward practical man.

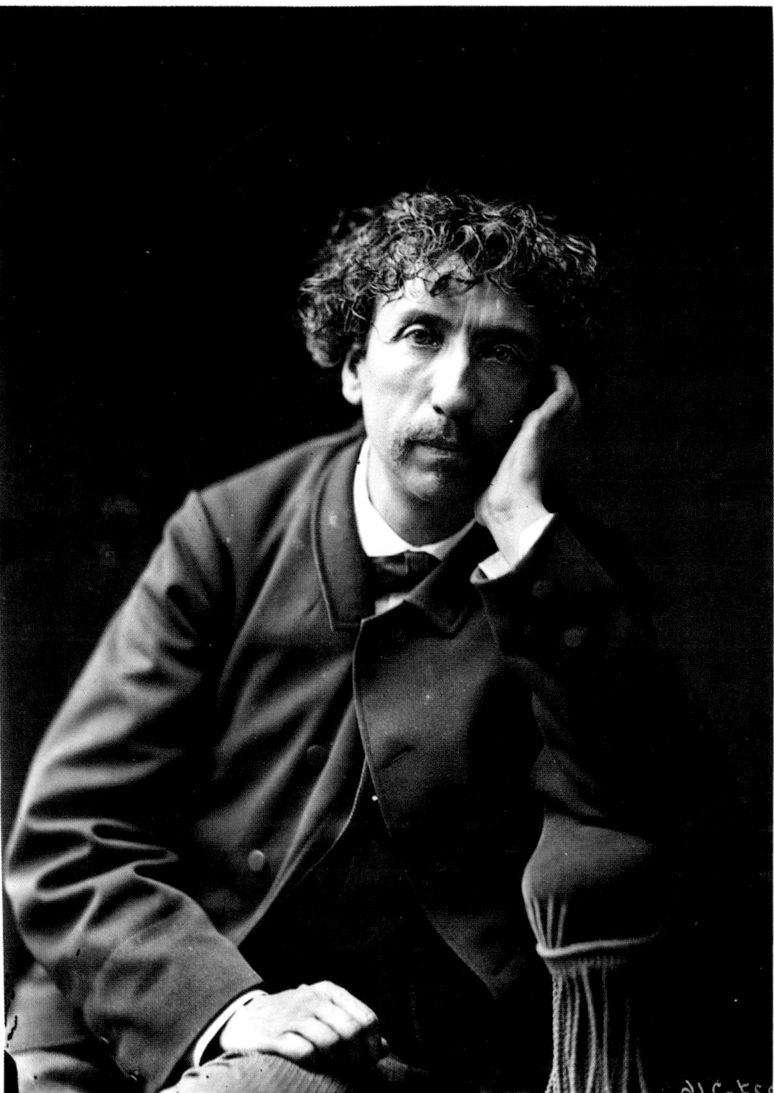

Victor Hugo, Paris, 1885. Nadar photographed Hugo (1802–85), an old friend and one of France's greatest literary and humanitarian figures, on his deathbed. Hugo's political beliefs led him to live in self-exile on the island of Guernsey for nearly twenty years following Napoleon III's *coup d'état*. His voluminous output included *Les Misérables* (1862), the story of an individual's struggle for redemption. Deathbed photography was common in most practices, but other than in exceptional cases such as this one, Nadar would send an assistant.

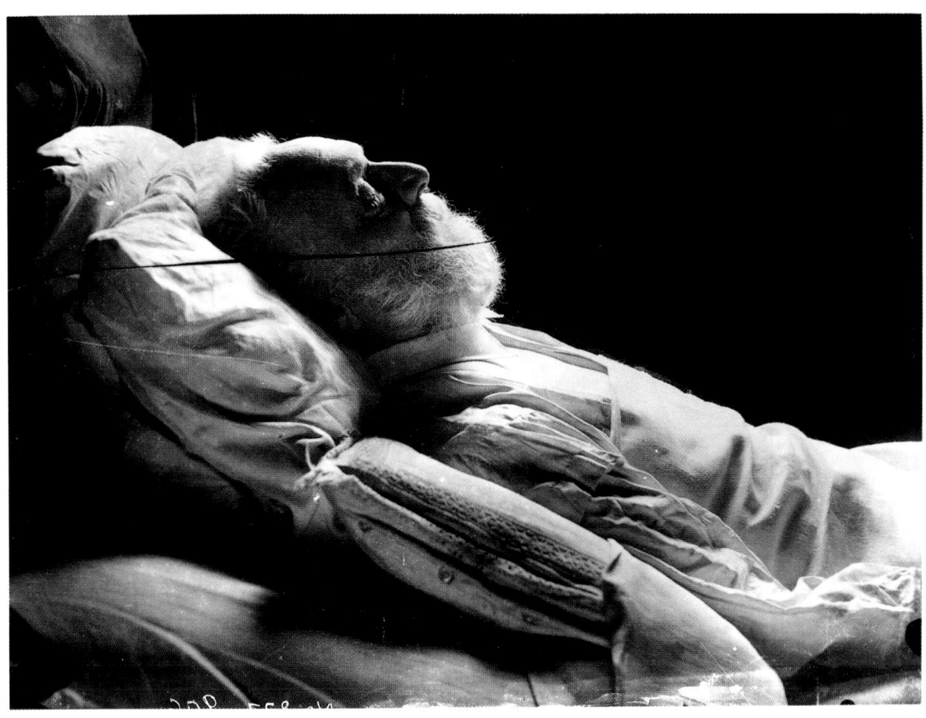

Discussion between Nadar and Michel-Eugène Chevreul on his 100th Birthday, Paris, 1886. In 1886, Nadar came out of semi-retirement to do a photo interview with the chemist Michel-Eugène Chevreul on his 100th birthday. This is one of a series of twenty-seven photographs, each accompanied by an excerpt from Chevreul's statements. In this particular frame, Chevreul claims 'I am far from denying what I cannot explain, but I would say that it must be proven to me, that I must see.' Chevreul's writings on optical phenomena had been of great influence in the arts. Nadar's portrait seems almost a caricature of the arrogance of old age, yet also a tribute to Chevreul's continuing vitality and self-confidence.

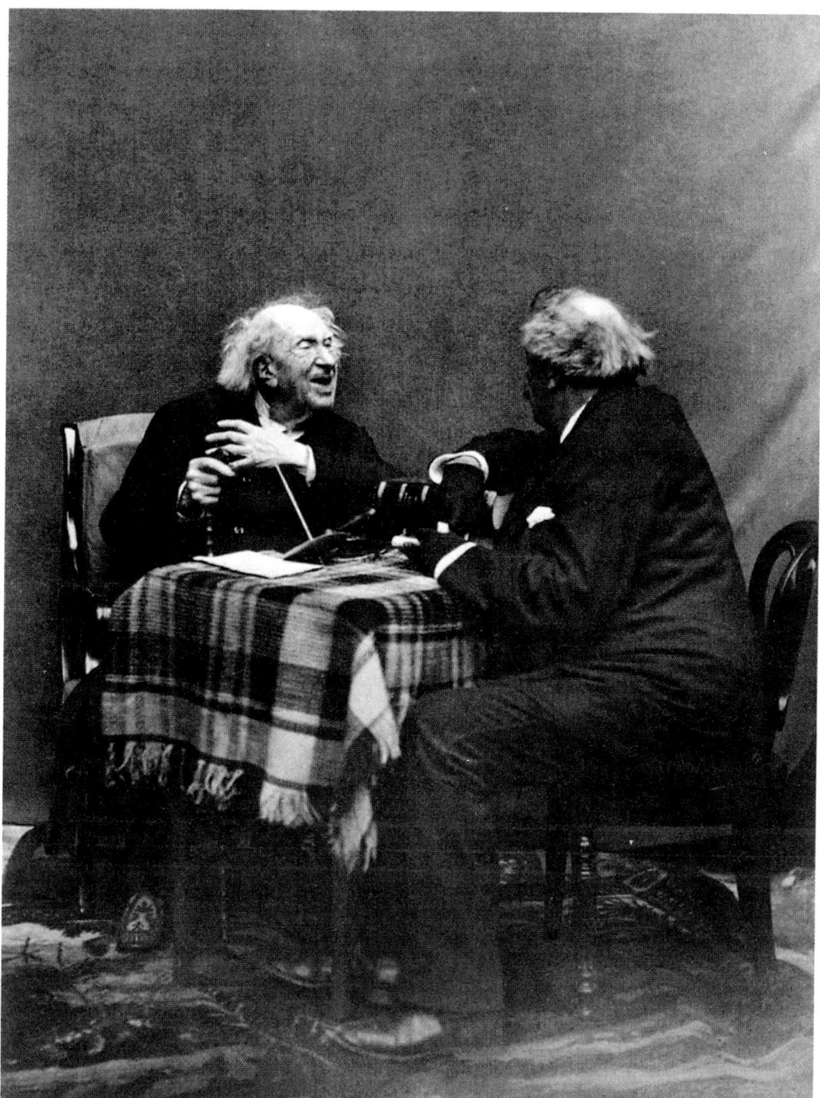

1820 Born Gaspard-Félix Tournachon in Paris to Victor Tournachon and Thérèse Maillet.

1825 His brother Adrien Tournachon is born.

1826 Marriage of his parents. His father's printing business continues to have difficulties.

1833 His father is forced to close his press.

1837 Death of his father. The family moves to Lyon, where Félix begins medical studies.

1838 Félix moves back to Paris. Takes the name Nadar and begins writing for various reviews.

1840s Associates with literary bohemians, including Charles Baudelaire. Begins publishing caricatures and consequently becomes the focus of police surveillance.

1848 Revolution breaks out. With his brother Adrien, he sets out on a military expedition to liberate Poland, but is arrested and returns to Paris in June.

1849 Begins close collaboration with Charles Philipon, publisher of satirical journals. This partnership is to last more than ten years.

1850s Continues throughout this decade and the next to publish memoirs and essays.

1853 Moves in with his with his mother at 113 rue Saint-Lazare.

1854 Publishes the *Panthéon Nadar*, containing caricatures of many famous contemporaries. Sets up his brother Adrien in the photography business and collaborates with him in running it. They photograph the mime Deburau. Nadar marries Ernestine-Constance Lefèvre.

1855 Has major argument with his brother Adrien. Nadar begins operating as a photographer from a studio set up at his mother's house. Sues his brother overthe use of the name Nadar.

1856 Wins first in a series of legal actions against Adrien. Joins the Société Française de Photographie, where he will exhibit many of his portraits.

1858 Takes the first aerial photographs, which he attempts to patent. Takes the first photographs with artificial light.

1860 Death of his mother.

1861 Opens a large studio at 35 boulevard des Capucines.

1863 Becomes interested in heavier-than-air flight and collaborates on the launching of the balloon Le Géant.

1864 Begins photographing Paris sewers.

1870 Outbreak of the Franco-Prussian War. Uses the balloon for reconnaissance missions.

1871 Paris Commune is formed. Nadar begins aerial postal service. Closes his studio on boulevard des Capucines.

1870s Begins to withdraw from photographic practice and settles in the countryside.

1878 Helps to organize an exhibition of the work of his friend the caricaturist Honoré Daumier.

1880s Continues to publish memoirs and essays.

1891 His son Paul Nadar takes over his business and founds the journal *Paris Photographe*.

1909 Death of Ernestine Nadar.

1910 Death of Nadar.

1950 His studio is dispersed. Approximately 60,000 negatives are given to the Caisse Nationale des Monuments, Paris, and prints, with other archives, to the Bibliothèque Nationale de France.

Photography is the visual medium of the modern world. As a means of recording, and as an art form in its own right, it pervades our lives and shapes our perceptions.

55 is a new series of beautifully produced, pocket-sized books that acknowledge and celebrate all styles and all aspects of photography.

Just as Penguin books found a new market for fiction in the 1930s, so, at the start of a new century, Phaidon **55**s, accessible to everyone, will reach a new, visually aware contemporary audience. Each volume of 128 pages focuses on the life's work of an individual master and contains an informative introduction and 55 key works accompanied by extended captions.

As part of an ongoing program, each **55** offers a story of modern life.

Nadar (Gaspard-Félix Tournachon, 1820–1910) was the most influential photographer of his generation. He is perhaps most famous for his series of outstanding portraits made between the mid-1850s and the 1870s, in which he created a lasting and affecting image of the French cultural elite. His concentration on faces and his Romantic glorification of the individual were crucial elements in his successful style.

James H. Rubin teaches History of Art at the State University of New York, and at the Cooper Union. He is well known for his work on nineteenth-century French art. His books include *Courbet* and *Impressionism* in the Art and Ideas series, and *Manet's Silence and the Poetics of Bouquets*.

Phaidon Press Limited
Regent's Wharf
All Saints Street
London N1 9PA

Phaidon Press Inc.
180 Varick Street
New York NY 10014

www.phaidon.com

First published 2001

ISBN 0 7148 4059 9

Designed by Julia Hasting
Printed in Hong Kong

A CIP record of this book is available from the British Library.

Photographs by permission of: Bibliothèque National de France; Photothèque de la Ville de Paris; CMN, Paris; Réunion des Musées Nationaux, Paris; The Metropolitan Museum of Art, New York; J Paul Getty Museum, Los Angeles.